craw

c r a w

Chris Apanius: Bass

Rockie Brockway: Guitar

Neil Chastain: Drums

Zak Dieringer: Bass

David McClelland: Guitar

Joe McTighe: Vocals

Will Scharf: Drums

Reissue Production by Hank Shteamer

Book Design by Aqualamb

Image Credits

Millie Benson: Photos & Artwork on pgs 6-7, 10-11, 13, 21, 25-26, 36-37, 39, 56-61, 67, 101, 115, 180

Derek Hess: Artwork on pgs 81-83, 127, 141-142

Erik Howle: Artwork on pg 116

Stephen Kasner: Artwork on pg 96

Andgeliko Marusic: Artwork on pg 200

Keith McClelland: Photos on pgs 30, 91, 140, 143, 181

Are Mokkelbost: Artwork on pgs 154, 165

Karen Novak: Photos on pgs 5, 12-13, 22, 35, 65-66, 71, 73, 93, 112-113, 130-131, 135, 168-169, 180-181, 183

Karen Ollis: Photos on pgs 166-167

Anastasia Pantsios: Photos on pgs 12, 32, 46-47, 85, 92

Arnel Reynon: Artwork on pg 101

Aaron Turner: Artwork on pg 172

Patrick West: Photo on pg 180

Second Printing: Edition of 300

ISBN: 978-0692565735

aqualamb.org / northernspy.com

CONTENTS

PADDY

So of course the citizen was only waiting for the wink of the word and he starts gassing out of him about the invincibles and the old guard and the men of sixty-seven and who fears to speak of ninety-eight and Joe with him about all the fellows that were hanged, drawn and transported for the cause by drumhead courtmartial and a new Ireland and new this, that and the other. Talking about new Ireland he ought to go and get a new dog so he ought. Mangy ravenous brute sniffling and sneezing all round the place and scratching his scabs and round he goes to Bob Doran that was standing Alf a half one sucking up for what he could get. So of course Bob Doran starts doing the bloody fool with him:

– Give us the paw! Give the paw, doggy! Good old doggy. Give us the paw here! Give us the paw!

Arrah! bloody end to the paw he'd paw and Alf trying to keep him from tumbling off the bloody stool atop of the bloody old dog and he talking all kinds of drivel about training by kindness and thoroughbred dog and intelligent dog: give you the bloody pip. Then he starts scraping a few bits of old biscuit out of the bottom of a Jacob's tin he told Terry to bring. Gob, he golloped it down like old boots and his tongue hanging out of him a yard long for more. Near ate the tin and all, hungry bloody mongrel.

And the citizen and Bloom having an argument about the point, the brothers Sheares and Wolfe Tone beyond on Arbour Hill and Robert Emmet and die for your country, the Tommy Moore touch about Sara Curran and she's far from the land. And Bloom, of course, with his knockmedown cigar putting on swank with his lardy face. Phenomenon! The fat heap he married is a nice old phenomenon with a back on her like a ball-alley. Time they were stopping up in the *City Arms* Pisser Burke told me there was an old one there with a cracked loodheramaun of a nephew and Bloom trying to get the soft side of her doing the mollycoddle playing bézique to come in for a bit of the wampum in her will and not eating meat of a Friday because the old one was always thumping her craw and taking the lout out for a walk. And one time he led him the rounds of Dublin and, by the holy farmer, he never cried crack till he brought him home as drunk as a boiled owl and he said he did it to teach him the evils of alcohol and by herrings if the three women didn't near roast him it's a queer story, the old one, Bloom's wife and Mrs O'Dowd that kept the hotel. Jesus, I had to laugh at Pisser Burke taking them off chewing the fat and

Bloom with his *but don't you see?* and *but on the other hand*. And sure, more be token, the lout I'm told was in Power's after, the blender's round in Cope street going home footless in a cab five times in the week after drinking his way through all the samples in the bloody establishment. Phenomenon!

— The memory of the dead, says the citizen taking up his pintglass and glaring at Bloom.

— Ay, ay, says Joe.

— You don't grasp my point, says Bloom. What I mean is. . .

Sinn Fein! says the citizen. *Sinn fein amhain!* The friends we love are by our side and the foes we hate before us.

The last farewell was affecting in the extreme. From the belfries far and near the funereal deathbell tolled unceasingly while all around the gloomy precincts rolled the ominous warning of a hundred muffled drums punctuated by the hollow booming of pieces of ordnance. The deafening claps of thunder and the dazzling flashes of lightning which lit up the ghastly scene testified that the artillery of heaven had lent its supernatural pomp to the already gruesome spectacle. A torrential rain poured down from the floodgates of the angry heavens upon the bared heads of the assembled multitude which numbered at the lowest computation five hundred thousand persons. A posse of Dublin Metropolitan police superintended by the Chief Commissioner in person maintained order in the vast throng for whom the York Street brass and reed band whiled away the intervening time by admirably rendering on their blackdraped instruments the matchless melody endeared to us from the cradle by Speranza's plaintive muse. Special quick excursion trains and upholstered charabancs had been provided for the comfort of our country cousins of whom there were large contingents. Considerable amusement was caused by the favourite Dublin streetsingers L-n-h-n and M-ll-g-n who sang *The Night before Larry was stretched* in their usual mirthprovoking fashion. Our two inimitable drolls did a roaring trade with their broadsheets among lovers of the comedy element and nobody who has a corner in his heart for real Irish fun without vulgarity will grudge them their hardearned pennies. The children of the Male and Female Foundling Hospital who thronged the windows overlooking the scene were delighted with this unexpected addition to the day's entertainment and a word of praise is due to the Little Sisters of the Poor for their excellent idea of affording the poor fatherless and motherless children a genuinely instructive treat. The

craw: an appreciation

"I've been trying to find a way for the terror and the beauty to live together in one song. I know it's possible."

—*Sonny Sharrock*

I DIDN'T KNOW I WAS LOOKING, OR WHAT FOR. IT WAS 1994, AND I WAS 16... That music could embody stagy darkness, brute ugliness was a given. The stylized gothic font of the *Headbanger's Ball* logo. The volcanic majesty of a Trey Azagthoth solo. Glenn Danzig's bare chest.

Another vista opened up through literature, film, painting. Learning to read Faulkner, Rimbaud, Henry Miller. Narrative extremity, fervent poetic flow. Learning to watch Jarmusch, Fellini, the Coens, to love the grotesquerie of Schiele, the weird hush and poise of De Chirico.

The idea that there was a bridge between these worlds would've seemed silly, beside the point. The sweat, volume, vulgarity of punk and metal lived over here, in the concrete basements and divey clubs. Books, movies, artwork belonged there, in libraries, museums, living rooms.

There was a zine in Kansas City called *FeH*. It was a bible to me. I saved interviews with bands like Morbid Angel and Cannibal Corpse and read them over and over. One issue featured a review of *craw*, the self-titled debut by a band of the same name. The author seemed genuinely unnerved by the record, its atmosphere, its imposing 69-minute length. The piece ended with a warning—something to the effect of "Hide all knives and other sharp objects before playing this record"—that seemed to be only partly a joke.

I will never forget those first weeks spent with *craw*. The disbelief and confusion. This music embodied the same aggression, the same will to overwhelm and conquer the space through which it rang out, that I knew from my metal records. But it seemed to access that other hemisphere of culture as well. The one where words and images, as opposed to slogans and stock iconography, mattered, where subtle, painstaking detail packed more of a wallop than screamed profanity. Uncanny scenarios glimpsed, revealed in flashes but never fully illuminated.

The ruthless order of metal was there too, but it was bent, mangled. Riffs that lurched wildly, stabbed at irregular intervals. Whirring, gaseous, disorienting leads. Shrieks to freeze your blood, offset by whines and mutters, the expressions of what seemed like actual disturbance rather than its histrionic counterpart. Stories not of blind rage but of curious detail. A spurned lover who "destroyed the paint job on my car." A three-year-old who "left the faucet on in the trailer and flooded the whole shebang." A pipe bomb exploding in the car of real-life environmental activist Judi Bari, "[driving] the nails up through the driver's seat."

Where did these stories come from? Why the odd specificity, as though the narrator had been poring through microfiche? What was this new aesthetic that accessed an entire mansion's word of moods—the dark, musty corners, hidden doorways and tangled histories—whereas what I'd known before had never bothered to move beyond the grand, well-lit entryway?

Lost Nation Road, album two, exploring another wing. Less violent, more murky. The sound of spiderwebs and muffled moans. The words taking on a new kind of fever. Oaths, visions. ("I've become pure speed, pure war." "They say snake people are special." "The solicitor man done told me / That the strongest human bond / Is that of twins / So that if one is accidentally maimed / The other will be all the more compensated.") Saxophones appeared on two songs, turning craw into a renegade mini orchestra, hurtling through crazed rhythmic obstacle courses. Voices bubbling up, strangled cries from all corners of the sonic field. Riffs of gnarled elegance. An exquisitely spooky ballad, "Bypass," that built from a soothsayer's whisper to a maniac's howl. A finale, "As Long as the Turnpike," that perfectly matched the elegiac poetry of the album title.

And *Map, Monitor, Surge,* a strange neon behemoth of an album. Rocking and rollicking in a whole other way thanks to new drummer Will Scharf's fluid, flailing attack. Sci-fi mini capers, spastic inventions, sardonic proclamations bordering on black comedy. A sneer had crept in, a sense of the band standing atop the rubble and letting a cracked grin spread across its collective face. Nuclear waste turned to glass; a containment specialist likewise "vitrified." Motel-room sex gone nightmarishly wrong. Secret file cabinets opened, gushing out data, evidence of cover-up, corruption, collapse. Song structures that zipped and darted and exploded into blizzards of raw sound, or sprawled with eerily epic contour.

Overload. Just like when I saw the band onstage—ceremonies of fierce, demented genius, enacted, frustratingly, for near-empty rooms. When I played these records, I felt menaced and enlightened, stupefied and serene. Pure content. A resonance that has carried on through two decades. Not just the terror and the beauty: the crunch and the chaos, the whine and the wail, the gag and the grace, the document and the disturbance, working on ears, mind, body, antennae. It was all there, then, and here it is, now and ever.

--HANK SHTEAMER
AUGUST, 2015

craw: an oral history

CHRIS APANIUS
(b. December 21, 1968, in Pensacola, FL; raised in Cleveland, OH)

ROCKIE BROCKWAY
(b. January 19, 1970, in Corning, NY; raised in Buffalo, NY)

NEIL CHASTAIN
(b. August 14, 1969, in Greenfield, IN; raised in West Lafayette, IN)

ZAK DIERINGER
(b. February 22, 1972, in Pittsburgh, PA; raised in Wheeling, WV)

DAVID MCCLELLAND
(b. April 8, 1970, in Boston, MA; raised in Needham, MA)

JOE MCTIGHE
(b. July 3, 1965, in Mitchell, SD; raised in Rochester, MN)

WILL SCHARF
(b. March 11, 1964, in Hastings, NE; raised in Berea, OH)

CAMEOS: STEVE ALBINI, DARIN GRAY, DEREK HESS, AARON TURNER.

Note: For details on all recordings mentioned below, see timeline/discography that follows.

I. Beginnings

ROCKIE BROCKWAY: So probably one of the very first records [I had], and I think it was a 45, was the Bee Gees, probably when I was 6 or 7, followed very closely by a Kiss 45. For the next couple years, there was just a mish-mosh of your typical late-'70s whatever was popular on the radio. I did get into a lot of Kiss—*Destroyer* and *Alive* and *Alive II*.

I didn't have any real focus until probably around 9 or 10 when the person that my mother was dating gave me a guitar. He was a blues guitar player in the region where I grew up, which was Buffalo. He gave me a guitar and said, "Learn how to play, kid." I'd go through his vinyl collection and listen to stuff, but apart from real basic chords, I pretty much taught myself how to play.

But the one guitar-tablature songbook that I had that I really learned how to play was a Zeppelin songbook. It covered probably Zeppelin I through *Houses of the Holy*. I learned every single song in that book, and that gave me an appreciation for the source music, blues and all that stuff, as well as a very deep appreciation for a lot of the heavier music.

DAVID MCCLELLAND: At my parents' house, there was very little music. [Their record collection] had come to them from Larry Trask, who was an American linguist that moved to England, and when he moved, he left his records to my parents: all the Beatles records; the rest of it was classical and weird British comedy like Flanders and Swann. The Monkees on TV were huge for me.

I took guitar lessons [from when I was 8] until I was 12, until my teacher, who was a nice guy, started having me sight-read jazz charts for songs I didn't know. I was like, "This is no longer fun," and he was like, "Well, what do you want to do?" And I was like, "Fuck if I know."

I remember I had this little tiny amp, which is an Alamo. I had this total crap guitar, a wood-tone electric, that had a Western styling carved into it. And I had this little Alamo, which I wish I still had, but if I turned it up enough, it would distort and feed back. So I was like, "Well, this is alright." And I had a Vox bass, which I got from my great uncle, and I could play that through the Alamo because it was so shredded, it didn't matter.

So I was sort of doing that just for kicks, and then my teacher basically broke up with me. He was like, "You're not practicing. I don't want to be your teacher if you're not practicing." I felt a little bad about it, but on the other hand, I was like, "I'm not going to practice. I don't want to do it the way you want me to do it; I don't want to be George Benson. There's stuff out there that you don't know about that I barely know about, and that's way more cool to me than this." So I stopped taking lessons.

At a certain point, [some friends] and I formed a band that was directly trying to be the Blues Brothers. These are the two songs we played: the *Peter Gunn* theme and "Green Onions." That's all we played, and we just would play them over and over. So I played bass in that. There were two trumpets, because we'd seen *The Blues Brothers* and we loved it, and we're like, "That's what we're going to do." That didn't go anywhere, for obvious reasons.

There was no school structure to fit this in. There was no jazz band; there was no instrumental stuff going on. Maybe there was a marching band, but all of us were in the school chorus. So I actually credit the school chorus with teaching me a lot of basics about music, about rehearsal, about listening, about going for an effect and figuring out how to achieve it. Because our teacher was pretty on it, and he was temperamental, like, "No, no, no! Do it again!" And we were singing real stuff; we were singing Fauré and other contemporary composers. So there was a lot of work that went into that project.

CHRIS APANIUS: My mom's side of the family is very musical. My mother was an orchestra director. I played lots of instruments growing up. I played cello, piano, bassoon for 12 years, through grade school. [I was] just sort of very immersed in it.

I read music for all the grade-school years. I think I started playing trombone in first grade, and I played all the way through high school. I played trombone in the band, and I played in jazz band; I played trombone, cello and bassoon in the orchestra. All kinds of stuff.

I was interested in classical, jazz. I was really big into classic rock through grade school. My uncle is a professional jazz bass player, so that was a big influence. Any music, all kinds of music.

What was fun is, in high school, the band director put together these brass choirs. I went to this Catholic high school, so we'd play services with a quartet or quintet in a cathedral and that was fantastic. And the jazz band would play out every other week senior year, which was a lot of traveling and playing.

NEIL CHASTAIN: At a pretty young age, I was very interested in drums. My father is a musician also; he played trumpet for a number of years. He played in the Purdue marching band in West Lafayette, Indiana, where I spent most of my childhood. For years, I asked for drums and lessons. I had a couple of those cheap drum sets you get out of the back of the Sears catalog that had the paper heads. So they'd last for a couple weeks or a couple months and then they'd break, and I'd be back to drumming on pots and pans. From what my mom tells me, I had a nickname from when I was really young and that was Thumper, because I used to bang on stuff.

I do remember pretty distinctly my dad giving me a football helmet when I was probably 3, maybe 4. But I immediately took it off, put it between my legs and started playing it like a bongo drum. So he quickly gave me a set of bongos; the first set of drums I ever had was a red-glitter set of bongos that I recall drawing on and trying to repair the heads with nail polish just to keep them from breaking. But I had those for years.

My first love of a band, believe it or not, was Kiss. My cousins both were drummers. So they inspired me a lot, and I wanted to play drums too. When I was 10, I started taking lessons, and then I think around a year after that, I joined a junior fife-and-drum corps called the Voyagers. And then I just kept going.

KITCHENS
AHEAD
HIWATT
NOISE IS THE SIGNAL

ZAK DIERINGER: For the first five years of my life, I'd drive to my grandparents', and my dad had two tapes in his car: the Beatles' White Album, which was awesome, and some Rolling Stones album, which I wasn't as excited about. I really liked the Beatles because they were good sing-alongs. So that was probably a huge, mind-opening thing, being a four- or five-year-old kid listening to "Revolution No. 9" and not thinking anything about it. I'm sure if an adult was listening to it, including my dad, they'd be like, "This is the weirdest thing ever." But to me, it was just another song on this album that I sang all the songs on as a little kid.

That was really music for me for a long, long time, until probably when I was in sixth grade, I saw Devo on the show *Square Pegs*. I didn't care much about music or listen to the radio, but that was something where I was like, "Wow, I've got to have this." So that was the first tape I ever bought with my own money: *Oh, No! It's Devo*. That was probably very important; it certainly made a huge impression on me.

I was in band in school, played the trumpet. In high school, I was in jazz band, and that's when I began playing the bass. That was sort of the beginning of my performing. I got into bass because I actually had a skateboard, and I broke my arm, and my mom wasn't going to let me skateboard. So I had a lot of downtime. I was still skateboarding, just without her knowing it, but I had a lot of time when I would've been skateboarding with nothing to do, so I got a bass.

The reason I got a bass was that my next-door neighbor was a super-good guitar player. In one year, he went from picking up the guitar to playing the whole Randy Rhoads thing and getting into really hard stuff after that. I was like, "There's no way I can possibly do that; I'll get a bass guitar because it seems a lot easier."

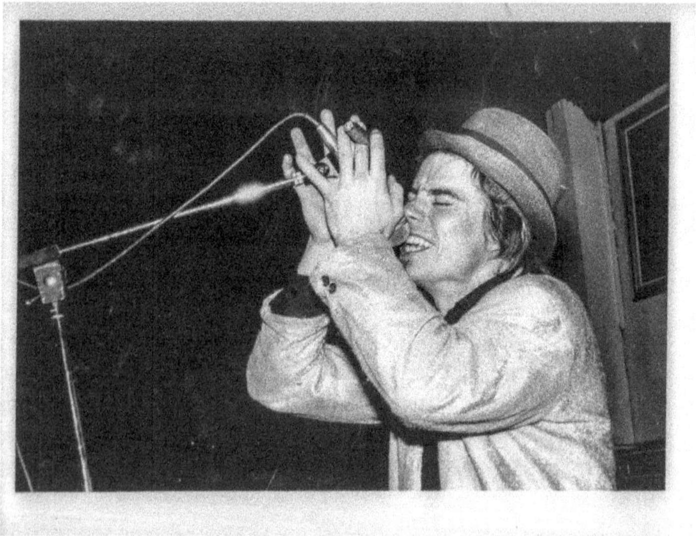

JOE MCTIGHE: As a kid, I heard everything my dad played, which ran the gamut from outlaw country to Sly and the Family Stone. A friend of the family played Scott Joplin on the piano, which I really loved. As a teenager I listened to an unhealthy amount of Pink Floyd's *The Wall*.

I was a mediocre trumpet player in grade school that became an average tuba player in high school. Our Catholic high school raised money for the music program by outfitting a swing band, which I played bass in. The swing band played mostly weddings, with plenty of sight-reading an enormous folder of sheet music.

I was reading constantly, but no writing. Toward the end of high school I decided that I couldn't be a Catholic anymore, which wasn't easy. There was a considerable amount of time reading to try to find an alternative path. I actually thought I could read my way out of the problem. At this time I was reading James Joyce and all the existentialists, mostly Kierkegaard and Camus. I also searched for any role model where the subject turned away from a mental construct that preached certainty. I put this time in "Slower" [from *craw*]: "I turned away from the herd into the unwelcoming arms of the absurd."

WILL SCHARF: I came from a musical family. My folks were both professors of music. They both graduated from Eastman, which was a pretty badass school for music. But we're completely opposite: I was into rock, because I was a kid, so that's what I was exposed to.

I was a total introvert, nerd kid when I was in elementary school and junior high school. I was the kid with the braces and glasses that nobody wanted to talk to. Dressed funny. I'd wear a plaid shirt and a plaid pair of pants and have these giant, geeky glasses.

So I spent a lot of time at home, and I was building models of stuff in the basement. I'm sure I was getting wasted off model-building glue when I was 11 or 12 years old. I was listening to rock, but I never really went out of my way to buy records or find stuff. And then one day, in the basement, I heard "Kashmir" by Led Zeppelin, and I was like, "What the fuck is this, dude?" I paid close attention to it. It's a long song, so it was an agonizing nine-minute wait till the end of the song for the DJ to call out the name. And I was like, "Holy fuckin' crap, that was awesome." And I think I went out that day or the next day and bought the record, and that was pretty much it. I was a Zeppelin convert after that.

I started playing, I think I was 16, when my folks got me a $200 drum set for Christmas one year. It was a snare, one tom and one ride cymbal. There was no hi-hat, and it was the worst set of drums you could possibly imagine, but I was like, "I'm gonna play everything John Bonham did." And about a year later, I went to a drum lesson. My folks set up the lesson; they were like, "You gotta go take a drum lesson, kid." I think I took two or three lessons, and I kind of lost interest. I guess I wasn't coachable, or something. I was like, "I just wanna play what I wanna play, man." I don't know if I figured it out, but I figured out what I wanted to do on it, if that makes sense.

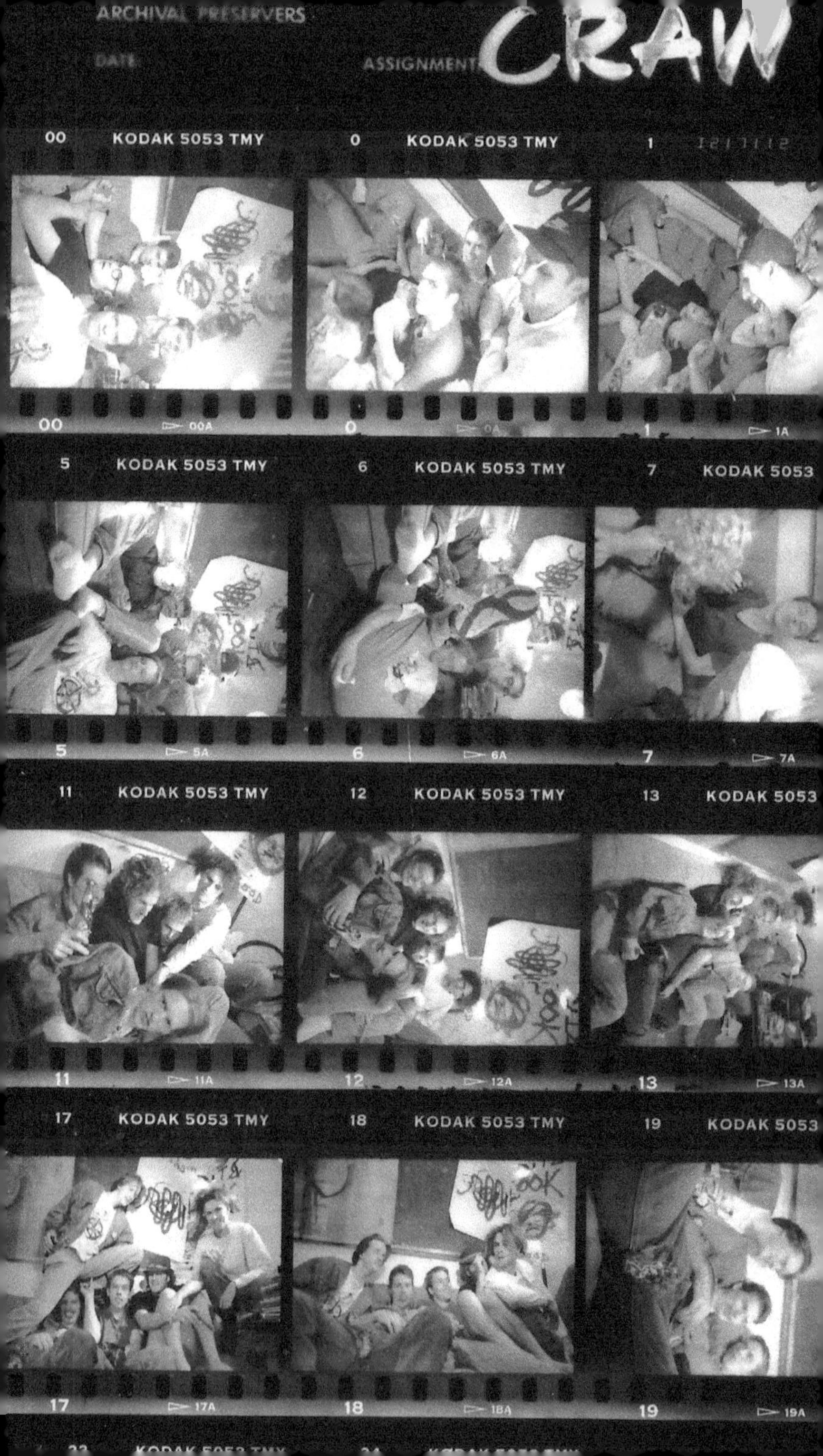
ARCHIVAL PRESERVERS
DATE:
ASSIGNMENT:
CRAW
KODAK 5053 TMY

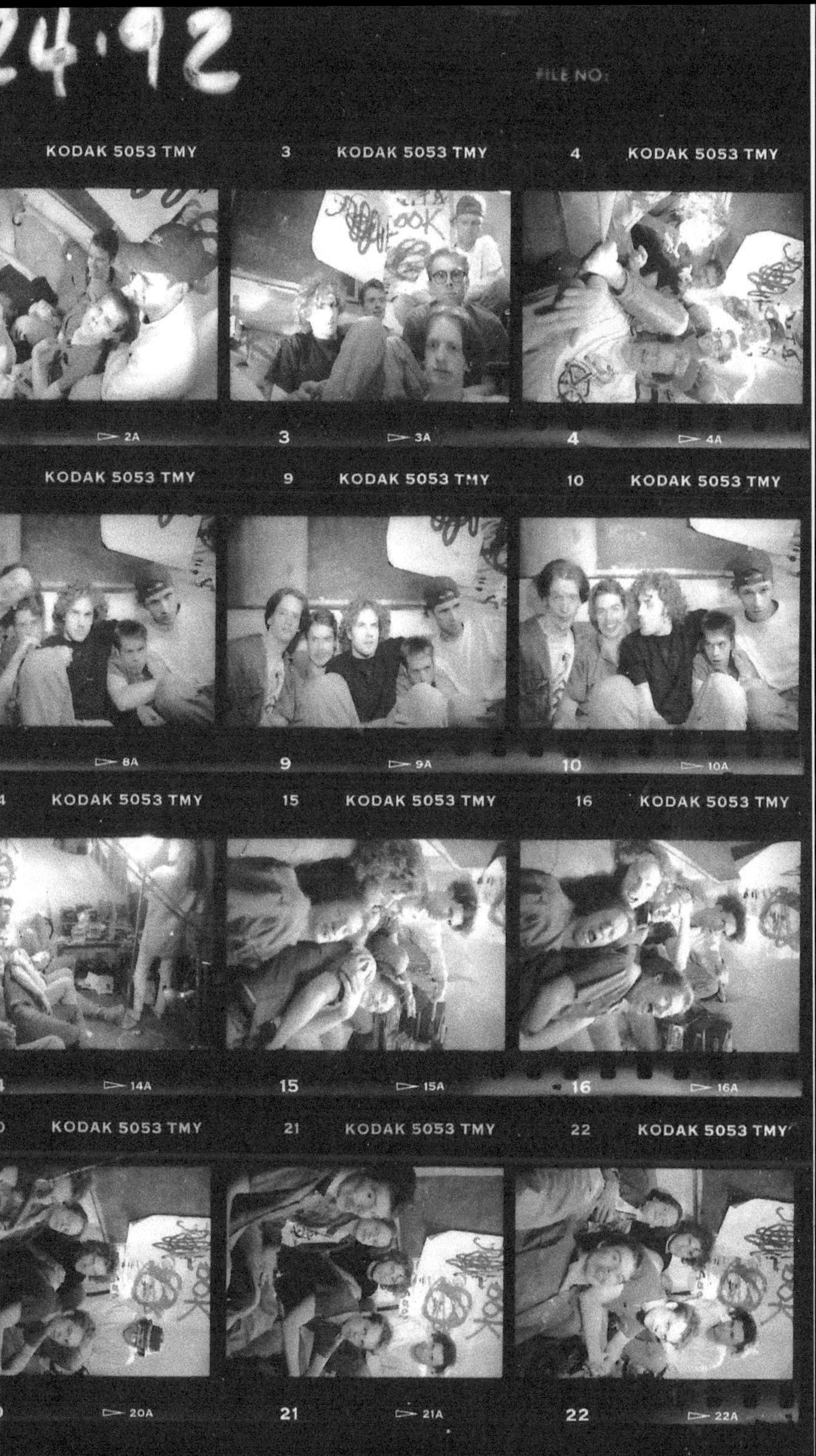
24·92
FILE NO:
KODAK 5053 TMY
3
KODAK 5053 TMY
4
KODAK 5053 TMY
2A
3
3A
4
4A
KODAK 5053 TMY
9
KODAK 5053 TMY
10
KODAK 5053 TMY
8A
9
9A
10
10A
KODAK 5053 TMY
15
KODAK 5053 TMY
16
KODAK 5053 TMY
14A
15
15A
16
16A
KODAK 5053 TMY
21
KODAK 5053 TMY
22
KODAK 5053 TMY
20A
21
21A
22
22A

II. Punk, etc.

CA: In high school, there was plenty of heavy rock—thrash, hardcore, punk rock and stuff like that. The first band I played in was hardcore. We played this show in Toledo with this band that was pretty well known. Nobody showed up to the gig. I was hanging out with a bunch of straight-edgers and hardcore rockers. I was also into heavy metal, thrash metal, death metal, all that good stuff: Cro-Mags, Corrosion of Conformity, Slayer.

A lot of the [shows were], instead of at a club, it was at somebody's house, and people would show up and you had a little show in the backyard. With the hardcore thing, we went to play a VFW in Toledo. We played at some venues, but it was more ad hoc. Essentially, I was playing music I was into with the people I was hanging out with.

My brother [Matt] is actually a great percussionist. His focus was the marimba and steel-drum band, but during high school, he played in rock bands, and I would play once in a while with them. He was the fastest and most skilled drummer I had known. Senior year and college, he was playing in this band in Kent called Hyper as Hell. They were just fantastic—heavy, dark, crazy, eclectic. So there was a lot of playing with my family and different people and different circles. It was all over the place.

DM: My second year [of high school], I met this kid who had a leather jacket and was into punk rock. He had the Butthole Surfers' *Locust Abortion Technician*. And then I met this other kid who was very into the Ramones. We started a band called Wet Love Debris, which at its most brilliant had two drummers and two singers, and we covered some Ramones song and [Misfits'] "Teenagers from Mars" and "Sex Beat" by the Gun Club, and we played a song that I wrote.

During that period, I saw the Ramones at Lupo's in Providence; I saw the Cramps at Lupo's. I would go back to Boston and see whoever could be seen—saw Hüsker Dü, saw the Butthole Surfers at the Channel. [The Butthole Surfers show] was overpacked, and there were so many people that I, weighing whatever I weighed, could lift my feet off the ground and still be supported by the crowd. And the fire and the whole thing—it was great. Saw Sonic Youth at Lupo's and at the Channel.

We kind of missed out on all the classic Boston hardcore. It existed and we heard it, but SSD wasn't playing when we were there; Jerry's Kids wasn't playing. Saw Angry Samoans a bunch of times. Saw Gang Green, which was great.

RB: No bands in junior high and high school, but I was introduced very early on to a lot of the punk rock and alternative music going on, because a close friend of ours was a freshman at the University of Buffalo who had his own college-radio program. We got involved in helping him book bands coming through Buffalo. When I was 15, 16 years old, we had 7 Seconds, Verbal Assault, Dag Nasty, all these great bands. We'd help set up shows in these churches or VA halls. That was great—being immersed in a scene at that age when you're figuring out what you like and your sense of direction and your musical taste.

I would take a cassette tape and listen to college-radio shows that were doing a lot of punk rock and just tape them. I actually have these ancient cassette tapes in my attic that have teeny little scrawled notes I made: "Gang Green."

When I was 16, I was teaching canoeing in a camp a number of hours north of Toronto. In between camping sessions, a bunch of us went down to Toronto and we were vinyl shopping, and this buddy of mine from Trinidad and Tobago was buying up *Ride the Lightning* and *Master of Puppets* and whatnot. I found an import of Corrosion of Conformity's *Animosity*, which totally changed my life. That record, for all intents and purposes, completely opened my eyes to the level of intensity and complexity that music can have. It was just a groundbreaking record for me.

JM: I was a Johnny-come-lately to underground music. In the mid-'80s we would road-trip the 90 miles to Minneapolis to catch shows, mostly at First Avenue / 7th St. Entry. Before moving to Minneapolis I was in a power trio called Hollowman that had a papier-mâché singer. We placed a speaker in the mouth of the hollowman and played a collage of vocals through it. Later I spent a year in Minneapolis and roomed with two record-store guys who would kindly comp me tickets to shows. That year was an education and a sense of a found community.

I was lucky enough to see Scratch Acid at the Uptown in Minneapolis in the spring of 1987. What I took away from that show has influenced me more than I care to admit. Slovenly's influence was more subtle, more of an encouragement that anything's possible. In the same vein, the Fall provided the evidence that great songs could be based on a word-drunk, come-all-ye approach to lyrics.

ZD: This is high school, 10th and 11th grade. My neighbor that played guitar, his older brother was into Rush, so we really [got] into Rush too. And [my neighbor] went off into more guitar-wizard, Satriani-type stuff, which I hated, and I was going off into a more metal, Metallica-type area. So despite being next-door neighbors and best friends, we never really played together. All my skater friends listened to punk rock, and I didn't like it because I thought it was crappy musicianship. I was more of a metalhead, and then somebody played me the Bad Brains and that was a huge, huge life-changer. The Beatles' the White Album, Devo's *Oh, No! It's Devo* and then the Bad Brains. It made me go, "Oh, I guess I need to pay more attention to this punk-rock stuff, because it's not all just crappy musicians playing crappy instruments."

And at the time in West Virginia, cool music was filtering in, but not a lot of information, so I really didn't have any idea when I was listening to Minor Threat that they were the same age as me and making records. They were, like, 16 years old; I thought they were 30-year-old guys, like everyone in a band was an old person who knew how to play his guitar. I just had no concept that, "Oh, these are just kids who just picked up their instruments last week and they're making records—I could do that too." I'd never really thought about being in a band, or taking music all that seriously or making my own records, because it just seemed like what older people did. I didn't really understand punk rock, and I just wasn't getting the information that I needed.

At the tail end of high school, I actually sang in a mostly cover band, kind of normal alternative music, like R.E.M. and the Smiths and stuff. That was my first rock performance. Even though I played bass, there I had a bass player, and I was like,

"Oh, I can sort of sing." So I did that for a while.

I went to Marshall University in Huntington, West Virginia. I was a psychology major. As a bass player, when I went to college, I went through my horrible Primus phase. Listening to lots of different stuff. I liked a lot of the normal college-rock stuff, like R.E.M. and Violent Femmes and stuff like that. I'd kind of stopped listening to metal, and at some point in there, I discovered Clockhammer. I don't know how I even heard about them. I think there was actually an article in *Alternative Press*. It just sounded more interesting and progressive, like what I'd listened to growing up but wasn't listening to at the time, and I found the CD and really dug it. It was a combination of alternative college rock, but with more foreign songs than what I was listening to. Different changes. Certainly more progressive than what I was listening to.

And I had a band called War Within. Awesome name! It was actually really interesting. We were just kind of all over the place. The drummer and the guitarist were both into Queensrÿche, who I couldn't stand, but they were really good players. The singer was more into Mr. Bungle and stuff like that, and at that time, I was getting over my Primus fixation and was more into Clockhammer, and I think Tool had just come out, their first full-length. So we were actually a heavy band with progressive leanings. Some of it was really neat.

WS: I started listening to Black Sabbath, and somewhere down the line, I heard Judas Priest, and I got into that stuff. I was a bad kid in high school; I didn't go to class. So I wound up repeating my junior year of high school, and I went to a school for bad kids in Maine. When I was in that school, I started getting exposed to other stuff that I hadn't really been exposed to very much, because everybody where I was from was into rock and metal. I started hearing jazz when I was up there, and I was like, "Holy crap—this is awesome." All different kinds of stuff: fusion and stuff that now I'd call Fuzak, and it's totally cheesy and stupid, but back then, when you first hear it, it's like, "Holy shit—these guys are doing this with their instruments?"

My first year of college, I hooked up with this guy Bob that I used to know from high school back in Berea—he was a big Rush fan—and this other kid named Steve, who was a prodigy bass player. He was in ninth grade or something at the time, but he was a monster player on bass. We wound up playing a bunch of Rush songs.

Then somehow, I hooked up with some R&B guys and I started playing in these R&B bands around Cleveland, jazz bands and stuff. A lot of it was just to make money, because the music was stuff out of *The Real Book*. You're playing "Autumn Leaves," "Girl from Ipanema," all these crappy tunes that everyone plays over and over again that kind of suck, but it's what the people want to hear, so you play it, and you get the paycheck at the end of the night. I did that for a few years.

And then in '89 or '90, somewhere along there, I started working at this jazz club called Club Isabella in Cleveland. And I was kind of always into weird music, but there was a lot of stuff that was out there that I didn't know about. I started meeting people like an old friend of mine, Tony Urso. He was instrumental in getting me into weird shit, man. He was a total punk-rocker; he was in this band called Starvation Army, and they toured a lot at that time, and I used to go over to his house and he used to play me records. I was like, "Wow, this shit's crazy, dude. It's pretty awesome."

So my collection of weird records started growing, punk rock and weird shit like that. I was also working with this girl named Becky Yody, and she was in this band called Sleazy Jesus and the Splatter Pigs, and they were looking for a drummer, and she convinced me to play with the band. I played with those guys for a couple years. That band never toured, but we did a lot of local stuff. The shows were pretty legendary in their weirdness and their ability to piss anybody off who was outside of the punk-rock circle.

A friend of mine named Ant Petty started playing in that band, and we started playing in other bands together. By the time we were all said and done, I think we were in five or six bands together within a two-year period. We started another band called 10 Tons of Hell that went through, like, 15 members. Eventually Rockie wound up being in it; that's how I started playing with Rockie.

NC: I moved on into high school, and I got more and more serious about music. I took lessons for about three years straight. Around age 13, all of a sudden hip-hop hits, and I want to breakdance and DJ and I start collecting hip-hop records. So my influences were varied. I went from Kiss to Rush, who was the next band that I really liked. My dad finally convinced me that Kiss really isn't that good, and when *Permanent Waves* came out, my dad bought it. My dad's a record collector, so he exposed me to a lot of music growing up: jazz, rock, funk, fusion. He loved Chicago, the early stuff, the first two albums. That was stuff I heard a lot growing up.

I did the drum-corps thing, and then I really got into classical percussion. All along, I did a little bit of drum set here and there. I guess my first real experience being around serious music study at a very high level was when I went to the Interlochen national music camp in 1986 when I was a sophomore in high school. It's an eight-week intensive camp. I ended up going to that three summers in a row: '86, '87, '88. My senior year of high school, the '87–'88 year, I went to Interlochen, so I lived up in northern Michigan. At that time, I was playing in percussion ensemble, orchestra, symphonic band, concert band, learning how to play marimba pieces and concertos and solo percussion pieces, and preparing for auditions. That's when I chose to audition for the Cleveland Institute of Music as well as many other schools.

III. Case Western Reserve; Cleveland, Ohio; Fall, 1988–Fall, 1990

CA: I was on North Campus; Dave was also on North Campus. We met at school orientation. Dave was kind of wild-looking. I could see who all the geeks were; I could see who all the rockers were, just by the quality of the T-shirt and the kind of T-shirt. I think early on I ran into Dave. I might've been walking to the cafeteria and we bumped into each other, and I was like, alright, he's a rocker dude. "Hey, dude, what's going on?"

We went to the Pink Pig, or something—it was [an] orientation at a Case farm off campus. Rockie walked by. He was wearing a COC T-shirt, or maybe Cro-Mags—something with the skull. And I'm like, "That dude's a skater. He's got the shirt; he's got the hair; he's carrying the board, and I need someone to skate with this weekend." Because Dave wasn't really a skater.

And you know, "I play bass; he plays guitar; what do you play? You play guitar? Perfect!" This is a match made in heaven. I've got my social life planned for the next month, with the guys anyway.

DM: I went to orientation, which happened in Thwing Center—I can even remember the room. I remember looking at this line of kids and everyone's signing up at these tables, and just looking around and being, like, "Ah, fuck. Here we go again with not being able to connect with anybody." And then I saw Chris with his Grateful Dead shirt, but a shaved head and a bandana, and I think he had his skateboard with him. And he had his brother with him, who also looked sort of punk rock. And I was like, "This is college; this is real life. I'm actually going to approach the person who looks interesting and talk to them." So I talked to Chris.

We meet up the next day, and then we went somewhere where there was a baseball field. And the way I remember it was, Rockie was wearing his cut-off jeans and a Melvins shirt, and he was, like, drawing in the dirt—squatting in the dirt, wearing his Sambas. And Chris was like, "That guy's got a Melvins shirt on." That's probably more true [that it was a COC shirt]. Chris is like, "Let's go talk to that guy." "Alright." Talk to that guy and we all play music: "Let's all go play music." So we get together in the basement of the dorm that Rockie lived in.

RB: So freshman orientation, it's basically me knowing nobody. There's all these people. I'm just kind of scoping the crowd, and I see this dude with short hair, kind of tall, hanging out with this long-haired kid. The tall, short-haired dude has a Corrosion of Conformity T-shirt on, and it ended up that [he] was Chris Apanius, and the long-haired dude was Dave McClelland. They had met maybe the day or two before; I think they were either in the same dorm or in dorms next to each other.

It was basically like, "Hey, I play guitar." "Hey, I play guitar too." "Wow, maybe we should play sometime." "Okay, let's do that." It was just one of those things that happened.

If I remember correctly, we never really tried to start with cover songs. Almost immediately, we were just like, let's see what happens. I remember a number of times where it was just the three of us, no percussion, and we were just playing dorm parties our freshman year, and people would come by, and we'd be playing these songs that we wrote. They weren't necessarily crazy-complex, but they weren't songs that anybody had heard of either. I would say that would be the start of the official craw response: "What the fuck is this?" People coming in for two minutes and then being, like, "Okay, whatever."

CA: Rockie set up an extra space in the dorm, and the three of us start playing in an empty dorm room or a utility room; I don't know what it was. This was on South Campus. We were writing songs and putting stuff together from the get-go.

RB: We had run into Joe a number of times. Joe was living on the same side of the campus that I was. I began noticing that people would mistake me for him, which is silly, because he's way taller than I am. But it turns out that we were clothed the same way. We both had jeans and black wingtip shoes and a green pocket T and a black overcoat. We didn't really know each other, but [people] were mistaking [us for] each other. And when finally we met, we were both like, "Oh, that's weird."

We ended up running into each other at a number of shows, one of which was Rapeman. Then we just kind of hit it off. Joe's the kind of person that when you meet him, you realize he's very literate, kind of intense, but a weird intense, kind of laid-back. He really knows specific things, literary, etc., and that was very interesting to myself and Dave and Chris, so we kind of conned him into agreeing to sing with us. We didn't even have a real band with a drummer or anything at that point. We were basically like, "You should sing for us." "Uh, okay." Kind of just thinking that if he just agrees with us, we'll go away. But we didn't, and one thing led to another.

JM: I saw Rockie around campus and knew of him. My friend Mohan sat down by him at dinner because Rockie was dressed in the same thrift-store starter kit that I usually wore. Rockie introduced me to Dave and Chris, as the three of them were skaters.

Reluctant singer is right.

DM: [Rockie and Joe] dressed exactly the fuckin' same. They had the same black raincoat. There was a difference in height. I think we sat down with Rockie and it turned out to be Joe, or something like that. Rockie probably talked to him more and asked him if he wanted to sing. This probably all happened at the lunch table in the cafeteria on the south side.

Joe had a guitar, and I think at a certain point, he was trying to play guitar with us and we were just like, "You know what? Get that thing out of here." He had this guitar that had three strings, and he was like, "I'm not going to tune it." He had spraypainted the whole thing black, and we were just like, "That's not a working situation."

CA: We bumped into Joe, who was dressed in a trenchcoat, or something like Rockie, except Joe's a lot taller. And we just started talking to him, like, "Oh, you're not Rockie. Who are you?" He was like, "I play bass." He's a really accomplished bass player, and we're like, "Sorry, Joe. We need a singer." He kind of just jumped into that.

DM: So we meet in the basement of Rockie's dorm, which is the dorm I ended up living in with Rockie and Joe. And we would play down there, and we didn't totally know this at first, but the sound would go up the elevator shaft. So we would play, distorted, and everyone [could] hear. That's also where they kept the pumpkins for Pumpkin Fest. So it was literally, like, a room full of pumpkins.

I don't know what Joe was singing through. Maybe that was Joe's amp—Joe had that shitty guitar and a Gorilla amp. We were meeting regularly. There wasn't really a point to it, but at the same time, we were all kind of putting a point to it by writing songs, bringing material, playing the same thing again. There was enough happening that we at least knew it was worth doing in the moment. None of us was ever like, "This is just a waste of time." It was fun; it sounded pretty good; it was interesting. We had our ideas that we were working on.

We could all go to to the deli and buy these six-packs of Drewrys. It wasn't, like, a low-alcohol beer; it was just a shitty beer that had less alcohol in it. You could just drink it all night, until at a certain point, you were like, "I'm pretty buzzed." And then we would stop playing and go out and cause havoc with the local wildlife.

There was always a party. So [playing music] slotted itself in. You meet, you jam, you drink, you go and drink more. It gave us that social nucleus that you need.

RB: I came across a flyer, which triggered a memory that "craw" originally started as "Corpse Retrieval Appliance Warehouse." I remember seeing a T-shirt with "corpse retrieval," [as in] scuba diving. It was kind of an internal joke with those guys. I honestly don't recall how it became Corpse Retrieval Appliance Warehouse and therefore C.R.A.W. I did find a flyer that actually had that name, and I was like, "Oh my God—I forgot about that."

DM: The name, again, came out of sitting in the cafeteria. Joe was involved; I think it was the four of us. We were trying to come up with a name. Rockie said, "Corpse Retrieval," because at his summer camp, the lifeguards called themselves the Corpse Retrieval. So I was riffing on that, and I said, "Appliance Warehouse." And I was like, "Oh, that actually spells a word; that spells 'craw.' " So that's why [our] early stickers have "C.R.A.W." That's how I remember it.

JM: I can't exactly remember why "craw." Partly based on the cliché that it's usually used in, but then I found that it was the crop of small bird, and I was sold. For the logo, I liked the rough type of the word "craw" in [the] 1946 Random House version of *Ulysses*.

RB: Eventually, sometime shortly after that, we found our first drummer, Lori Davis. Lori was at the Cleveland Institute of Art. For people who don't [know] the community around Case Western and University Circle in Cleveland, the campus has three or four major schools: Case Western, which is a combination of the Case Institute of Technology and Western Reserve, which is more the liberal arts side, and then Cleveland Institute of Art, with all the art students, and then Cleveland Institute of Music. So this would've probably been my sophomore year and her freshman year at the Institute of Art, and she was just this ridiculous drummer, this teeny little skinny girl with all this pent-up energy—just this powerhouse drummer. And that's when we started writing probably some of the early, early craw material.

DM: I remember going to [Lori's] dorm room to watch her "try out" for craw. Her room was empty but for a bed and her drum set. She might have been wearing her beret at the time. She sat down and attacked her drums and blew us away and was "hired."

CA: Somebody said, "If we want to start playing out, we've got to put a tape together." It wasn't long before we were trying to piece stuff together, and then we added [Lori]. We were writing songs. I think what I remember is we wrote some stuff we just bagged. We were filtering. I think that [1990] demo tape, we were trying to tune the songwriting and keep the better stuff.

DM: Pretty early on, we started bringing in music. I think Rockie was like, "I'm going to bring in some stuff." We would just jam, but we would also jam on stuff that we were working on that were ideas. A lot of those songs on the [first 1990 demo tape], the germs are Rockie's and then we would fuck with them in a certain way.

CA: The first year would've been in the first dorm, maybe in [Lori's] apartment, and then sometime near the end of the first year or beginning of the second year, we got down into the Staley [dorm] basement. I remember recording down there. That might've been the demo. That's where I remember putting together the tape cover and the paperwork. Somebody was making copies of the recording on tape, and we started peddling them. [The cover] picture came from my photography class, just a random picture. That's my youngest brother.

DM: The thing about the first [1990] demo is, all the ideas for craw are there. The odd time signatures, the abrupt changes, the roles of the two guitars, the general assault, the busy-ness, and especially Joe's vocalizing and lyrics. Those are complete songs, and Lori was a full part of it. It wasn't like we were showing her stuff and having to bring her up to speed; she had it, and it was great. She learned the songs, and I believe contributed a 5/4 groove to one of the songs. She might have contributed more, but that stands out as one of our first forays into odd time signatures.

We played at least three shows with [Lori]. We only stopped playing with her because she didn't come back to school after summer break. It's just a weird twist of fate.

CA: We played a few shows with Lori. I'm pretty sure Euclid Tavern was the first—I wouldn't be surprised if it was fall '89—and then we played Kent. We played in Kent at JB's Down, where I used to go watch all the other punk-rock bands—I knew people at JB's that got us in there. Having a "chick drummer" made us instantly popular.

[Lori] was killer; she was great. She went to CIA art school for a year and dropped out. She left for some reason. She's from Indiana; she went back home.

DM: The Hessler building was party central. They were these old, beautiful, huge apartments. There were, like, 9 million people living in one apartment, but they would be cut up in funny ways. And at the basement window—this was on a main street right through campus—right up against the window, you could look down and see someone's musical gear: a sampler, all this electronics stuff.

Rockie and I would walk by [this] window, and we'd look in and see all these synthesizers and sequencers and samplers, which at that time was all huge stuff. And we were like, "Wow, that guy's probably really cool. I wonder what's going on with him?" Finally, a friend of ours, Ron Kretsch, said, "Well, if you guys need a drummer, I know a drummer," and we went to his apartment, and it was the guy with all that equipment. That was Neil, and he was living there with Ron. So Neil, besides being a great drummer, had a huge amount of electronics experience. And in starting to work with him, we really started to take things more seriously because he was going to music school, and he was a professional musician.

NC: So what happened was, fall of '90, I leave CIM, and then I meet these guys. They come down to my apartment. I'm living in a sub-level apartment at 1961 Ford, still on the Case campus, and they had just lost their drummer. They had already started craw and played with [Lori Davis], another person from West Lafayette, Indiana.

As I recall, maybe my door was open, and these guys, like, literally walked into my apartment: "We hear there's a drummer around there." So we set up a jam, and we're like, "Ooh, this is cool; we're on to something." Rockie already had the crunch and was really good with his rhythm, and I had been playing drum set then for almost a year—six months to a year. I'd played as a kid, but [I was] starting to play with punk-rock groups. So we start jamming and honing some pretty interesting ideas. Really early on, I felt that this was something unique and something that I really wanted to be a part of.

IV. Sound

CA: The thing about Neil is, he's just a killer drummer. He's probably one of the best drummers I ever met, maybe aside from my brother. He was at CIM, so that's classical training; he's a drummer's drummer. And I don't remember exactly when, but then he went to University of Michigan for jazz training, which probably better suited his musical style and interests because he was just into doing anything and everything rhythmic. He was just into exploring every piece of it and every aspect of it.

With each new song, Neil wanted to try something new rhythmically. Every time he was playing, he was just exploring the free space. To me, it's not exactly just embellishing here and there and doing the fills; it's the rhythm, the counterrhythm and putting something in whatever little space there was.

RB: From a guitar player's perspective, [Dave and I came] from different camps. I know that a lot of his influences came from Robert Fripp or whoever else, on that very talented, intricate guitar-playing level. I didn't really have that specific interest while growing up; I really enjoyed that really thick, meaty riff playing. [The role of each guitar player] was something that was never really defined officially; it was just an evolution of what the band actually ended up being.

DM: At that point, I was completely obsessed with Sonic Youth. And there were other people that I was obsessed with that were in there—just the whole idea of the guitar as a very vocal instrument, a sheet-of-sound kind of instrument. And Rockie was coming from a very straight-ahead metal thing, and had those chops. He can drop the needle on an Iron Maiden album and play it. When I went to his house in Buffalo, it was like Iron Maiden records and posters, Sabbath, Zeppelin, whatever. He would just learn that shit—that very classic "Guy in his bedroom learning rock records on the guitar." You can hear it in his playing, and it's great. That was a very natural thing for him to do, and the other stuff was very natural for me, because it's just where my ear goes.

NC: The great thing about Dave was that he was the guy that always kept us from being a metal band. I always felt like Dave was that perfect left-field X factor on a lot of things. Then there were elements where he took over, but he also did a lot of great lead stuff. And he had his influences that I really liked. Dave was really into Sonic Youth and stuff like that, and I really liked that sound too. We all were pretty open-minded. Rockie had the metal background; he was more on the heavy side.

CA: I was into anything and everything but loved the heavy stuff. Rockie was into the heavy, chunky thing, and Dave [was] into the more psychedelic stuff, for lack of a better word, like Sonic Youth. So we just kind of threw it together. It turned out—I don't know if Dave and Rockie would agree, but Rockie filled the rhythm and Dave looked like what he was doing was sort of the lead in a traditional sense. So it's kind of a fun balance, and we were just loving it.

RB: From a composition perspective, I don't necessarily remember doing the whole full-on, "Let's jam and see what comes out of it." I'm sure that happened. I do recall everybody individually coming to the table with riffs, and then we'd learn the riffs and see what comes next. That historically was craw's methodology. When you really get down to the nitty-gritty, a lot of the craw material—not all of it, but a lot of it—came from one person. There were very few craw songs that came out of jams.

I would say that a good majority of the time, someone would come to the table with the majority of a song already down: "Here's riff A, we'll do that X times. Then we're going to go to riff B, blah-blah-blah," and map out most of a song. There's obviously room for creativity and all the other parts.

NC: A lot of the composition was done by everyone sort of coming up with their own parts. And often it was one person who had a road map already. Rockie would be like, "Check this thing out; I've got this thing." It could be a piece of a song; it could be one riff; it could be a whole structure. There were tunes that I structured entirely from drumming that everybody just riffed on and figured out what to do with. And I would repeat stuff until they would be able to sort out what they wanted. And we would all make suggestions to each other.

V. Word

JM: Generally one person would write the song and everyone else would layer over it. I would take direction from that person. Most times I had free rein over what I was doing.

I learned the songs through repetitive listening. I [made] notes, and had to count. After listening to the song on a cassette 10–20 times, I would then review the 5–10 sources I was reading at the time, and make a decision that one source would fit better than the others.

I took direction from W.S. Burroughs's quote about the "*naked* lunch, a frozen moment when everyone sees what is on the end of every fork." I would cast about for suppressed stories or alternate histories. More direction came from science or speculative fiction, where our hero is transformed by social or man-made environments.

DM: Joe's a brilliant guy. He was a musician. He played the tuba; he played jazz bass. I'm pretty sure he could read music. He kind of flipped a switch and said, "I want to bring some of these ideas to singing." Ideas from progressive literature, Burroughs cut-up ideas, the news.

JM: I reckon I just heard a compelling story and repeated it. Obviously there was nothing unique about this style, as I'd already heard Bob Dylan or Big Black do the same thing. Nonfiction material was an effective way to hang my emotional life on a structure. The process was to try to write a satisfying song, whatever that means.

Throughout everything I've done, there's been a theme of failure: social, technological, and personal. All three were grist for the word mill when it came time to scramble some lyrics together. When I used the personal, my priority was to what I thought the song needed over strict reportage.

The process was to simply react. Given a song fully realized, given the choice of lyrics for it, I would react, perhaps unconsciously trying to have the song have some coherent emotional arc.

The method was to write what I wanted to hear. I didn't have to make a career out of music because I had a degree to fall back on, so I didn't have to "sing" anything I didn't want to sing. I never had specific goals, which was evident to anyone who saw us in the early years. On the other hand, I never thought I needed to have one. At that point in history, I thought the requirements of a "frontman" were passe. Just because I was the one with the mic, I was required to engage the audience, to fill time while the band fucked around between songs. I didn't care if the audience was "feeling all right," or to present a coherent philosophy outside of the lyrics.

CA: [Joe's] a rocker kind of guy, but on top of that, he's also very well-read: James Joyce and some of those literary hard reads. I think a lot of what he used and a lot of what he wrote, I think he drew on that to put his lyrics together.

And of course, his stuff is just out-there. Very crazy. Like, wow, man. The feeling I get is, he certainly can convey some torment. Is that really what's in him or not? Sometimes it makes you wonder. But I think a lot of it comes from his literature reading. Over all the years, I've never really asked him about it. I think with the words, he's trying to magnify the feeling that you're getting from the music, put some context under that and it just blows up or something.

JM: I do find screaming somewhat cathartic; it may be one of the few times it's socially acceptable to do so.

During craw, I would play occasionally against the metal style to add tension, as the individual playing against the group. Burying the vocals was a means of subjecting the audience to an aphasic experience, where the vocals are heard but not understood, as they would be at most of our shows. I liked that "Aphasia" was the title of the first song on the first record—a signpost that what was to come.

As for practice, rarely did we bother with a P.A for the vocals. During most times I would sit, listen, and map words to song sections. Before a recording, often times I would be at home, with the Walkman on, listening to the cassette of the songs without lyrics and frantically trying to match one to the other, thinking myself a fraud all the while.

DM: The emotion that [Joe] would deliver was huge; it was intense. I think that sometimes, it would scare people. It was a couple iterations beyond where most people were comfortable listening.

STUFF AND NONSENSE.
BY
A. B. FROST
CHARLES SCRIBNERS SONS

PAUL
VIRILIO

SPEED
AND
POLITICS
Every person within the United States who is an agent of a foreign principal and required to register under the provisions of this Act and who transmits or causes to be transmitted in the United States mails or by any means or instrumentality of interstate or foreign commerce any political propaganda for or in the interests of such foreign principal (i) in the form of prints, or (ii) in any other form which is reasonably adapted to being, or which he believes will be, or which he intends to be, disseminated or circulated among two or more persons shall, not later than forty-eight hours after the beginning of the transmittal thereof, file with the Attorney General two copies thereof and a statement, duly signed by or on behalf of such agent, setting forth full information as to the places, times, and extent of such transmittal.

Jeff I've written in the back of this book because I couldn't find paper, didn't want to really look through your home for it but I desperately needed the release but for me show no living being this because this is a part of me no living thing knows but me + you now.

THE
TAO
OF
PHYSICS

this is written as it registers or enters my mine no order.

I'm dying! I know it and I'm not financially cable of saving my life I get a job to get a home + because I have no home I end up losing my jobs. I would leave work actually not knowing where to go going through my phone book trying to find someone's wife or girlfriend to lay (endulge sexually just to have a bed to sleep in so I would make it through work doing what they want and how (for me) doing artificial stimulants or masturbating just so that I would feel different not dwell

on my feelings because
I know I like everyone
else have a chance to see
tomorrow and in that itself
there is hope for change
Knowing all this
I'm still unhappy I know
I'm dying I am able to
change it and still haven't
Its been now exactly
1 yr + 15 days That I've
been trying + that I am
aware of my heath
problem. Its my problem
I've faced health Insurance
but no job or no home
no family reference
guarantee of payment etc [illegible]

I'm scared shitless to
ask a friend for financial
help they would want
reason I care not to say
I don't wish that feeling
of hurt pain on noone I
know what is like to hear
that someone you have
made part of you is
leaving permanently
when they haven't even
begun to live. I'm frighten
I want help + will accept
only if I can keep what
keeps me going which are
simply commense, balls (Guts)
sense of humor & my
freedom

potential, even knowledge
which is simply commen
sense. why do I hurt
and why am I afraid of
me. I don't want to die
I want to get better

pastel celery any of several types of commercially
Paschal celery grown celery having green
unblanched stalks.

patsy a person who is cheated, victimized, or made
the butt of a joke

peaked intr v ed, ing, s to become sickly,
emaciated, or pale

peek-a-boo A game for amusing a child, in which
one repeatedly covers and exposes one's face,
exclaiming "peekaboo!"
Adj made of a sheer or transparent fabric

pelorus a fixed compass card on which bearings
relative to a ship's heading are taken

adj peltry archaic paltry, petty, contemptible

pet[1] intr to make love by fondling and
caressing

pet[2] n A fit of bad temper or pique
intr v petted, ing, s
to be sulky and peevish

peter ed, ing, s to come to an end slowly,
diminish, dwindle
to become exhausted

pettifogger 1. a petty quibbling unscrupulous
lawyer

pettifogger 2. a person who quibbles over trivia

pettifog intr v to act like a pettifog

phony not genuine or real; spurious, false
something not genuine, a fake
A person who is an imposter; hypocrite

pigaback variant of piggyback

piddle to use trifling(ly); squander
to spend time aimlessly, diddle
2. to urinate

piffle intr v to talk or act in a feeble or futile
way
n foolish talk or ideas; nonsense

piker A stingy petty person, esp one who
gambles cautiously

pink[1] sympathetic with or influenced by
communistic doctrine

pip 1a a dot indicating a unit of numerical value
on dice or dominoes
b a spot or speck
4 A radar signal

pixy adj playful, mischievous

placket 1. a slit in a dress, blouse or skirt
to make the garment easy to put

bask awhile in my
sun

Social Darwinism
in humans is expressed
in the realm of
economics

Album Titles

Humours and ~~[illegible]~~
Tumors

Interrupt

Unexpected guests
Solving the problem of
Seduced by Empathy
Empathy leads you
the paths
The Many ~~Moods~~ of Empathy
Distracted by Empathy

TO THE CHILD READER.

Curious beasts, with paws and claws,
  Curious birds, with plume and feather,
Strangest freaks of Nature's laws,
  Here for you are brought together.

Owls and monkeys, pigs and bears;
  Humming-birds and toads and rabbits;
Hunt them to their nests and lairs;
  Study all their ways and habits.

Learn how the mosquitoes talk;
  Why the wasp and hornet sting you;
Learn the meaning of the songs
  Linnet and canary sing you;

How the beaver builds his dam;
  How the penguin feeds her baby;
Of the lobster and the clam;
  What their moods and manners may be.

All these things, when you shall know,
  Write a book yourself, my dearie!
For, so learned you will grow,
  All the world will flock to hear ye.

VI. The Euc

The CITY by derf
True Story
WALK
Crow
GROG SHOP
SAGRES
GRAB!
SAGRES
MAN... WALK IN THE CROSSWALK!! IF SOMEONE HITS YOU OUT THERE, YA DON'T GET NOTHIN'!!!
TIM WAS SO TOUCHED BY THIS SHOW OF INDIGENT COMRADESHIP THAT HE COULDN'T BRING HIMSELF TO TELL HIS MENTOR THAT, ALTHOUGH HE
LOOKED LIKE A FELLOW BUM, HE WAS IN FACT A GRAD STUDENT...
OH WELL... IT'S A FINE DISTINCTION ANYWAYS.
E-MAIL: DERFCITY@EN.com

RB: When I first got to Cleveland, it wasn't a really cohesive scene, so to speak. There were shows that would come through Cleveland, and we would hear about them. There weren't any real close clubs that did a lot of music we were all interested in, nothing that was really super close to campus until a few years later. So at the time—this was when we met Joe and those super early formative years of the band—it was really kind of like, "Hey, so and so's playing, let's plan on going out there in a couple weeks." It wasn't until '90, '91 that the Euclid Tavern really got off the ground and became really that nexus of a scene within Cleveland.

Derek [Hess] at the time was working in the kitchen at the Euclid Tavern. The Euclid was right on the edge of Case Western campus. At the time, Derek was auditing some classes at the Cleveland Institute of Art. He went to the owners of the Tavern and said, "Look, you guys don't have anything going on Monday nights, and nobody comes in here. Do you mind if I book a couple of bands every Monday?" And they said, "Sure, go ahead." We played a couple shows. It was all teeny little shows, because it was the very beginning of that scene. And then probably four or five months into it, '91, I would say, he booked Helmet, and I think for the Cleveland scene, that moment really kind of set the stage for a good number of years where the Euclid Tavern was just the place to be.

DEREK HESS: Monday nights is what I was given to book [at the Euclid Tavern], and it evolved into Mondays and Wednesdays, and then whatever days I needed. Because the bar was in a transition, and they were finding that they needed beer sales at the bar. And the bands they had been booking traditionally, their audiences had been growing up, getting married, having kids, getting DWIs, or not coming out anymore—these blues bands. And I was able to fill that void with bands that brought a lot of energy to the club, brought a lot of attention to the

club, and also generated the sales that made the owners happy enough to let me continue to do it. I was doing all the art for the Euc, because I was studying printmaking across the street at the Cleveland Institute of Art while I was booking there, so I was doing all the flyers for all the shows.

When I first started booking the room, craw were coming around wanting shows. Rockie was always pretty persistent about wanting to get gigs. I know that's how they got their first show. I know I put them on the local showcase, with three local bands. That way, we could see what everybody's about. And they were right there at the beginning, when I first started booking the Euc. I started in '89, and I don't know what year they started, but it wasn't much longer [before] these guys showed up at the doorstep. I would give them a show with a local lineup and be pretty impressed with what I was seeing. So eventually, I got craw to basically be the house band, and I had them playing at least once a month, generally in support of a larger touring act.

There was a resurgence going on in a lot of cities at the same time. Minneapolis had the AmRep thing going on; Chicago had the Touch and Go thing going on; the West Coast had Sub Pop and all that. Cleveland was struggling to find its own identity. And, I tell you what, craw showed up, and you can point to this band being influenced by this, and that band being influenced by that, but craw brought so many different elements to the table that you couldn't say craw sounds like this band or that band. They were their own thing.

They were young guys; they were hungry guys, and [there was an] amount of professionalism they brought to the table. A lot of the other bands that were playing Cleveland were playing for, you know, a 12-pack of beer and doing their thing, which was fine and all. But they were definitely not as standout as craw was.

They carried their own. For some reason, they really didn't break out of the Cleveland market. It wasn't for lack of trying. I think they could've been perceived at times as a difficult listen. Whereas you're listening to something that's really easy to snap your fingers to, craw was definitely a very technically sound band with tons of different ideas that they were bringing to the table. They weren't playing off in different directions; they were playing as a unit. But it was almost too much for someone who just wants to go to a club and sing along.

I was able to watch them grow, and each one of them was bringing a different level of experience to the table. Rockie knew his power chords, Neil was precise, and Joe was just kind of learning as he went along, but he had the passion. As the years went along, it was obvious that they went from rookie to veteran.

I can't remember a bad craw show. They were a big draw in Cleveland, and they wouldn't have been drawing that many people if they weren't good.

NC: Those [Euclid Tavern] shows were just kicking off when craw was formed. It was literally almost the same time. So within a handful of months of Derek Hess throwing his Monday night shows at the Euc, we were on some bills, because he was like, "These guys are a like-minded part of this." And we were influenced by what he was doing and we had our own influences as well. It's grunge-era, but we're not grunge; we were like this post-punk, Touch & Go, Amphetamine Reptile kind of band. And I think seeing Helmet at the Euclid Tavern—all of us I believe were there that night, the first time they ever came through Cleveland—was very inspirational too.

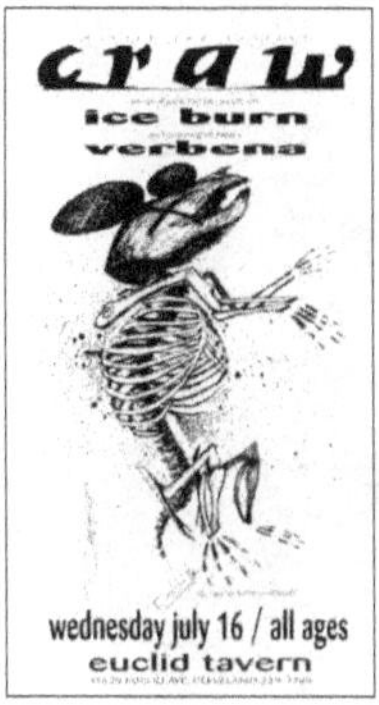

RB: There [were] absolutely a number of years, right before or right after that first record came out, where we were the house band at the Euclid Tavern, and we would open for some of the bigger acts that came through. We got to play with Corrosion of Conformity, Tar, the Melvins. For me, I wanted to play with some of these people that I really respected.

And one of the things I really dug about that scene at the time was, it wasn't just the scenesters that were coming out. We would have classical-music students at Cleveland Institute of Music come up to us and say, "I have no interest in any of this loud, independent punk or whatever you call it, but you guys are doing crazy shit." That was really neat.

人編成のオーケストラを結成、地元クリーヴランドの5人組でフリード自身がマネージャーを務めたムーングロウズ、その他ドリフターズ、ジョー・ターナー、ファッツ・ドミノらをレギュラー出演させた。

後年の出演者に、やはりクリーヴランダーのスクリーミン・ジェイ・ホーキンスがいた。彼は、このアリーナで行なわれていた地元のボクシング・コンテスト"ゴールデン・グローヴス"にも参加していたボクサーで、そのステージは、棺桶やヴードゥーのお護り、"ヘンリー"と名付けられたしゃれこうべといった小道具を使うことで有名だった。1957年、一連の"ムーンドッグ"のツアーと、アラン・フリード主演の映画『ミスター・ロックンロール』への出演によって、彼はそのキャリアの頂点に上りつめる。ホーキンスの役は、鼻の穴に骨を通したアフリカのブッシュマン戦士。これにはNAACP(黒人地位向上委員会)が激怒、映画会社に抗議してホーキンスの場面をカットさせた上に、全国棺桶協会にホーキンスへの棺桶提供を差し止めるよう働きかけるまでに至った。そんなこともあって、ホーキンスはその後ヨーロッパでの演奏旅行を余儀なくされたが、1977年、アラン・フリードの生涯を描いた映画『アメリカン・ホット・ワックス』に出演の機会を得る。またしても同じ役であった。

ここ、クリーヴランド・アリーナは、1972年、ジョージ・マクガヴァンの大統領選の資金集め集会の会場となり、ジェイムス・テイラーや、アート・ガーファンクルとのコンビを解散した直後のポール・サイモンが出演した。現在この建物はなく、地元の赤十字の本部が建てられている(3717 Euclid Ave.)。

ドローム・レコード・ストア

DROME RECORD STORE

ジョン・ドロメットことジョン・トンプスンは、70年代半ば、このクリーヴランド初のパンク・レコード・ストアをオープンする。当初の名前は"ヒデオズ・ディスコドローム"だった。12417 Cedar Rd.のショップは、まもなくこの新しい音楽シーンの中心となり、映画の上映や詩の朗読、パーティーなども行なわれるパフォーマンス・スペースの機能も果たして、ペイガンズやディーヴォもここで演奏した。ドロメットは、自らの"ドローム"レーベルからペイガンズのシングルを何枚かリリース、パートで働いていたデヴィッド・トーマスは、時間を見つけては自分のバンド、ペール・ユビュのレコードを梱包したり、ファンジン"CLE"の発行を手伝ったりしていた。その後ショップはウエストサイドの11800 Detroit Rd.に移転、さらに1290 Euclid Ave.に移転したが、不審火のせいで1980年に閉店する。ドロメットは現在LAで"インフォドローム"という会社を運営している(InfodromeのEメール：idrome@hollywood.cinenet.net.)。

ユークリッド・タヴァーン
EUCLID TAVERN

クリーヴランド出身のクロウ。"ユークリッド"にて

"オルタナティヴ・プレス"誌は、ダウンタウンから5マイルの位置にあるこの小さな店を、常に街で最高のクラブとして紹介している。月曜日と水曜日は、たいていの場合、無名のツアー・バンドをステージに上げており、土曜日はもう長いことヴェテランのミスター・ストレス・ブルース・バンドの独壇場になっている。15-60-75が町に来た時にプレイするのもここだ。何の飾り気もないこのタヴァーンは、天井の金属のシーリングも壊れているような細長く暗い店で、奥にゲームのスペースがある。1987年の映画『ライト・オブ・デイ』のある場面はここで撮影された。マイケル・J・フォックスとジョーン・ジェット、そしてエキストラでトレント・レズナーも出たが、話題としてはその程度の映画だった(11629 Euclid Ave., University Circle, TEL 216／229-7788)。

VII. Influence, method, gear

RB: There was definitely a lot of common ground. We were all very interested in some of the louder type music. Chris was funny, because he was a huge Cure fan, and I had historically been very anti- that whole movement of new-wave and emo stuff. But Chris also was a huge Slayer fan. Chris, probably more than anyone else at the time, got me to open my eyes and ears a little bit more, because he was a huge speed-metal fan and a huge [fan of] the Cure and all that other stuff. Chris's love of all music inspired me.

DM: So two really formative things happened to the band: One was Dave Earle, who used to write for *Alternative Press* or something, he had some radio connection, and he played us the first Jesus Lizard EP [*Pure*], with "Bloody Mary." And I already knew about Scratch Acid, but I didn't know about the Jesus Lizard. So he played us that first album and we were all like, "Oh my fuckin' God, this is the best thing ever." And then the Melvins happened. Rockie had maybe already been listening to them, but I think *Ozma* or whatever finally clicked, and he's like, "Oh, well, this is obvious—this is what we should be doing." Those two things happened, and then at a later date, *Goat* came out, and that again was kind of like, "Well, obviously we need to be moving in this direction."

The Jesus Lizard and the Melvins I feel like were very formative. They're obviously very different bands, but we were like, "We're gonna take these two things and just smash them together."

NC: [When I joined craw], I was combining my studies in classical music. You have to realize that when you talk about classical music in 1988, there's a lot of very contemporary, very challenging music that you're going to play. You're going to play shit that really makes people's hair stand up. And that was an influence too, the postclassical music that inspired me. There were little bits and pieces of things from Edgard Varèse that I used to steal, appropriate and throw in. Varèse was a big inspiration; Frank Zappa was an inspiration to a certain extent. We wanted to combine all of these things. Extremes were a really interesting thing.

And I think Einstürzende Neubauten was somebody I learned

about from Ron Kretsch. Ron Kretsch had a peripheral role [in craw] in a way. He was just an inspiring dude and art guy who got into music, and he knew about all this fuckin' crazy music. And so Einstürzende Neubauten, they used these dynamic extremes and these metallic instruments or found-sound percussion. Those kinds of things also inspired and informed me in the way that we approached craw.

So you talk about those extremely different textures and extremely different moods all in one piece, and conveying those emotions. It was pretty emotionally stirring and sometimes disturbing music. We definitely had a goal to cut into you and make you uncomfortable, but then sort of give you something along the way. We liked that. We were trying to dig through your comfort layers and make you feel something. We sort of burned your arm with a cigarette while we slapped you silly.

We tried to employ a lot of what I would call compositional devices to create some of those jarring effects. And a lot of that is sonic extremes and obviously dynamics. We loved to go from super soft to super loud. We also like rhythmic extremes and tempo changes, time changes, just anything to try to keep you off-balance at all times. We're not the only band that's ever done it, but we certainly did it in a different way.

RB: There's probably a number of sources that I could trace [the complexity of my writing] to. When you come right down to it, from my perspective, I'm a complete science and math geek, so I really enjoyed that relationship between music and numbers—to the point where I just wrote down prime numbers and mapped them out on the fretboard without even playing anything, and then actually made that into a riff. So to a certain degree, I could cite a Corrosion of Conformity or a Rush, but I think that the reason I liked all of that stuff is just because I'm a geek.

I'd play around with all sorts of stuff and map all sorts of things out on paper. [I had a] weird, cryptic way that I would document some of the stuff that I was writing, and that also gave me the ability to be mathematically creative with some of the things. So I could look at what I was drawing in terms of the fretboard and where I was putting fingers or what notes, and I could visualize other systematic relationships, and I could see if something could maybe work out of that and just kind of play around. A whole series of trial-and-error type of things.

DM: I think the successful things [I wrote] were probably improvising and then memorizing the parts of what I improvised that I liked. Sometimes I used tape, not that much. It was a faulty method, because I would write stuff and I would forget it; then I would write stuff and I would remember it and I would rehearse it enough that it would be a thing.

RB: I wrote a lot on my acoustic. I know better now, but with the drop-D tuning, I would do all these chords that span three or four frets that on an acoustic guitar sound amazing, but you lose it with the distortion on the electric. I was a real stickler for trying to document what I wrote because I'd always forget it. That was nothing more than diagramming out a fretboard and where I'm actually putting my fingers. And then if I knew it was going to be like a "123 123 1234," I'd document that.

As the music got more complex, a lot of that was myself coming up with, let's say, riffs in 13/8, like the end of "Elliot" or something like that. Or Neil coming up with rhythmically percussive craziness, like he played out a lot of the song "Cobray to the North," which was stylistically similar to a lot of the Brubeck 9/8 stuff. As the band started getting more into the complex region, a lot of that probably did source from the two of us.

I would come to the table with these riffs that ended up being polyrhythmic. I didn't know what the fuck polyrhythmic meant. Neil would actually be like, "Wow, you're just coming up with this off the top of your head?"

DM: That [1990] demo has odd time signatures in it. Something in 5/4, I forget which one, and the end of "[Onion Fucked-Out-Virus Ragman Targeted in Dizzyland Daisy Forget-Me-Not-March]" has a four-bar tag of 3/4. And there were other bands. Obviously, the Melvins were all over the map, so they're a good inspiration but not a good teacher. And I hate to say it, but Primus. A lot of Primus's shit is not in 4/4 and we all went and saw Primus.

And Neil did go to music school, and he had a deep musical education that the rest of us didn't. So we were bringing stuff to him, like I'm sure that he didn't hear the Melvins except through us. And he knew stuff that we had never known that was just part of his minute-to-minute thinking about things, so he was like, "Odd time signatures? They work like this. This is it. You want to play in 7, you do it like this." So he kind of threw that giant building block at us.

CA: A lot of it was that odd rhythm and the empty space. Traditionally, it's all about that riff and playing as much as you can, but it's pretty powerful when you hit what you're doing, and then there's the empty space. The empty space makes the [riff] more powerful, so that was that whole thing. That whole thing with the riff rock, playing the odd time signatures and all that, it sort of came about when we were sort of exploring... "How 'bout this riff? That sounded kind of cool, and it feels really funny, or it gives you this kind of feel that isn't your regular 4/4." A lot of that came out in the jams and the exploration. And at a certain point, it was, "What the heck are we playing? Is that 4/4? Is that 6/8? 3/4? 2/4?" "Oh, no, that's 13/4." Or "That bar was 7/8." And of course, Neil with his training was like, "Oh, no. That was 7/8, and the next bar is 13." And then we started thinking, "So we're doing all this—what is it?" And I guess that's sort of where the whole math rock, the geek rock [came from]... I guess we used to call it the math rock.

DM: After seeing the Melvins, Rockie got some new gear. He got a Dean Markley head. He had a Yamaha 4x12 cabinet with red speakers, and then he added another cab, which was two 15-inch speakers in one enclosure, and I was like, "I've got to step up my game." So I bought the Hiwatt [head], and it was a constant struggle to get a decent-sounding 4x12 cabinet. There was always the thing [in craw] about the low guitar and the high guitar, but I didn't want to be the high guitar in terms of having no low end to my sound. It was very, very difficult to get that balance. That Dean Markley that Rockie got has this signature low-end growl, so he nailed that right away. And Chris got the Traynor [head], and that was playing through six 10-inches, so he had a bigger sound.

It's just that thing when you're creating something cool. "We're getting it," you know what I mean? We're getting it together. We're pulling it from the places we're pulling it, but we're making it into a thing that is our own thing that's really exciting. When Rockie got that amplifier, I was like, "Holy fuck, that is a loud, cool sound—I have to step up my game." And when I did, I was like, "This is totally exciting. You can just go and buy new gear, and it sounds awesome, and it complements what that we're writing, which is also awesome."

NC: I had already for some time been using this double floor-tom set-up. It was a floor tom above my snare; it was like my first rack tom. I would usually have two more toms, so you'd have the floor tom on the stand angled back just above the snare drum, and then to the right of that, you'd have the highest rack tom, and then to the left of that, you'd have rack tom two. And then the floor tom on the right was rack tom four.

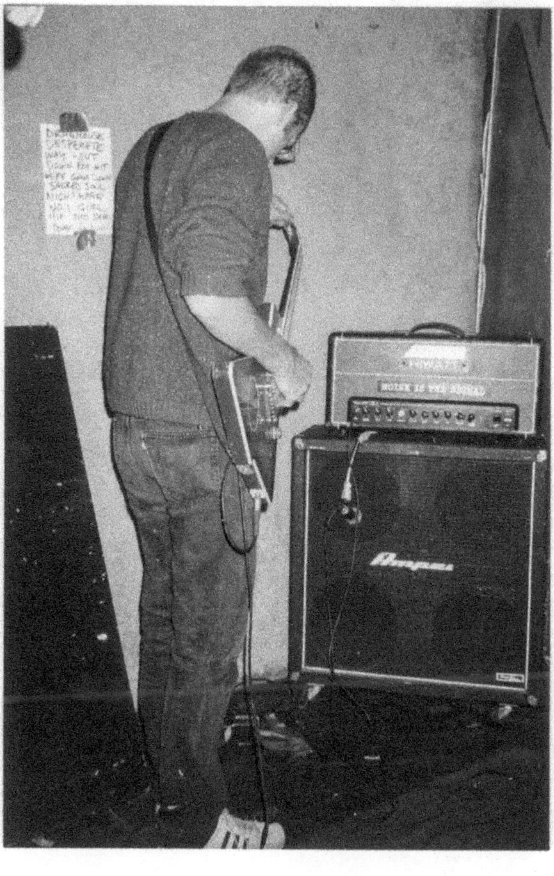

ROAD
QUE SIRHAN SIRHAN

Interlude: "405"

DEREK HESS: Everybody wanted to hear "405"; that was their hit.

NC: That song just came to me. It was one of those tunes where I knew what I was going to play [*sings opening pattern*]. Doing those double-floor-tom riffs with the bass drum added and then the snare just like flams. And some of that influence of some of the music that would punch and then be tight, and there would be a little blip of silence and back at you. So that was one of those things where I had come up with a structure and some pretty solid ideas, and when I brought them in, the guys loved it. Rockie went right for it.

RB: If I remember correctly, "405" was an example of Neil writing that first really staccato part, and then me listening to that and being like, "Wow, you know something? What if we went into that open part out of that."

JM: In "405," I start by redefining the number for the "sign of the beast" as a tip of the hat to metal and to acknowledge the ascendency of science over religion. I then repeat the two reasons why that year was the worst year of her life. Using the first person made it less like reportage.

405 breakdown

(wait two)

We are not allowed to give out
any information

(wait four)

Her face was frozen
and I knew (x3)

(wait one)

It was like I committed a crime
or something

(wait ~~4~~ → x2)

whenever I see him at work
I shake

VIII. craw

RB: It was definitely really intense rehearsals in Cleveland [leading up to the first album]. We did some shows here and there sporadically in that prep phase for that record, but it was mostly three times a week, as much as we could do to hammer out a) what songs we were going to play and b) to make sure we were actually going to be able to play them the way we wanted to.

CA: The whole thing was a passion. The type of music we were doing, it wasn't just jam rock; it was orchestrated. It's heavy rock played in a club, so really, how precise does it have to be? But by God, it had to be precise. I guess that was just us and what we wanted to do with it. We're going in and we want this to be really good and really well-orchestrated. There was a lot of time and effort put into that.

To me, to get ready for Albini, that wasn't any different than anything else. I think with a lot of things, we had a goal and we worked at each one of them. Maybe the intensity was a little more, but every next thing we did, it brought it up a level. I do remember that we spent a lot of time [preparing for Albini]. It had to be perfect.

DM: Between the [1992] demo at Mars and the first record, we practiced our asses off. We played more than a few shows, and we also just practiced like madmen. I don't want to overstate, but I think we would play three times a week, and we would practice on the weekends for a few hours. A few sessions for, like, four hours. We would spend a lot of time. Basically, we were like, "If we're gonna fuckin' do this, we're gonna practice a shitload because we're not going to get there and look like idiots in front of Steve Albini; it's just not gonna happen."

NC: Once a song was down and it was honed, we would rehearse it until it was perfect. And we rehearsed a lot. Sometimes every day of the week. Going in to see Albini? Six days in a row, five days in a row, practicing three or four hours a day to get ready for different stuff. So I think the band still to this day had one of the best work ethics of any band I've ever been a part of. Actually, I'm going to take that back; I'm going to say the best. And a huge level of sacrifice that everyone was willing to make. Not just with their time, with their lives. It was a unified vision: "This is what we're doing with our lives. Craw is what we do; craw is who we are."

RB: There were a couple guys in Cleveland—one of them worked at an area record store. [Someone told him,] "Hey, I know somebody who's putting together a label and they're looking for bands." And our friend who was working at a record store had seen our band and also knew what these guys were looking for because of their musical tastes and kind of set this up. We went to Youngstown to play a show, or Pittsburgh or east Ohio, where these guys came: Brendan [Coyne] and Phil [Tory]. They came, they saw, they liked, and then we started talking about what it would take to be this first band on this new little label [Choke, Inc.] that they were basing out of Chicago. It just kind of went from there.

The first craw CD came out in '93, so that couldn't have been any earlier than '92. It all went kind of fast after that. We already had that material recorded from [our 1992 demo], so we just put out that 45 with "405" and "Stomp." I remember there was the process of putting a contract together, which, hindsight being 20/20, was absolutely ridiculous for an indie band on a teeny little indie label.

It was pretty quick after that. Between Joe, Dave and myself being big Big Black fans and knowing that [Steve] Albini was recording, we were like, "Hey, you guys are in Chicago; Albini's in Chicago. Set us up." That was the funny thing, because when [Brendan or Phil] tried to call Steve, Steve said, "You're a record-label person, right? The band can call me." He didn't want to have anything to do with the record-label guys. I forget who called him. One of us called Steve and said [*mock-timidly*], "Hello, we'd like to record with you."

DM: Albini came to the Euclid Tavern playing bass for Flour. Rockie went up and gave him the tape [of *Celephais*], and said, "Hey, we'd love to record with you." And Albini got in touch with Rockie and said, "Yeah, you can come do this."

STEVE ALBINI (1997): The first album I recorded with craw, we did a double album's worth of material in three days. It was a real marathon. But they're excellent musicians; they came prepared.

RB: The first two records were recorded in Steve's house. It was almost like a level and a half. The actual studio itself was in the basement. It was super cramped. I remember the four of us—and this is pretty much standard throughout all of craw's recorded history—would play live together, laying down the initial tracks, and then additional tracks might be to beef up some of the riffs or add atmosphere, but the core of the songs were always recorded live with all the instruments. And I remember being in that teeny little basement studio just kind of having fun. It was a really fun experience both times, with that recording session and *Lost Nation Road*, at Steve's place.

The biggest thing I remember is that we recorded a ridiculously long amount of material [for *craw*], and we recorded it and mixed it in five days. And Steve was hating us. Not literally, but he was just like, "I can't believe we're doing this much." But we did it. We realized we had one day left and we realized we had to add a couple of additional tracks and do Joe's vocals and then mix all of it. We were like, "Oh, shit." We did it. We stayed up for 16 hours or something like that.

CA: Albini, that was quite an experience. That dude, I look up to him. And I think some of the other guys, with Big Black and all the recordings and projects [he did], were big fans. I'm a big fan of some of his music, some of his later stuff, so going there and working with him was by far one of the best experiences.

He had this set-up, and it was in his house. The recording studio was in the third floor or the attic, or maybe that was the second floor. So every time you'd lay a track down, he'd try to pipe it through some speakers, but to work with him, you had to run upstairs and go listen to it. It was very tight. Of course, we had big equipment. I guess if you're going to play heavy music, you need big equipment. But we did not fit in that basement. He had to baffle everybody for this recording.

RB (1994): His basement is set up within two rooms. There's a very open drum room and then the next room—you just walk through another door and there'll be the instruments. At times it can be a challenge just because our music tends to get slightly complex, and we need a lot of eye contact. Being in two different rooms, the only way we could see, looking at the drums, would be through this little narrow door.

CA: We didn't have a big space; we were tight in the basement. We couldn't see. So that was a little rough, because when you're playing this kind of music, there's a lot of visual cues, like, "Okay, we're coming in." You're watching for the white spaces, and you're watching for when to come back in and for the timing. So that was very difficult.

RB: I was the closest to the door, and I'd watch Neil if he'd have an actual visual cue to come back into the song. I'd have my guitar up so that the other guys could see me and then kind of come down.

CA: I think the recording went very well, but there's a few things that we had to lay over. To try to re-lay tracks just listening to the music versus having those visual cues, that was a little rough.

JM: I found Steve to be hard-working and honest, which is the highest praise a Midwesterner can give. We wore him out on the first record; the story I tell is that the band slowly fell asleep one by one, like the apostles at Gethsemane, while Steve mixed until the early morn.

The recording time was tight, and there wasn't time to re-work the lyrics over and over again. It was obvious to everyone in the studio when there was a song I wasn't 100% ready for, and we would re-do the vocals a couple of times, call it good enough and move on. The feedback was occasional, but I always listened. There was bit of an unspoken rule that everyone was responsible for themselves, and we didn't have many criticisms of anything but our own parts.

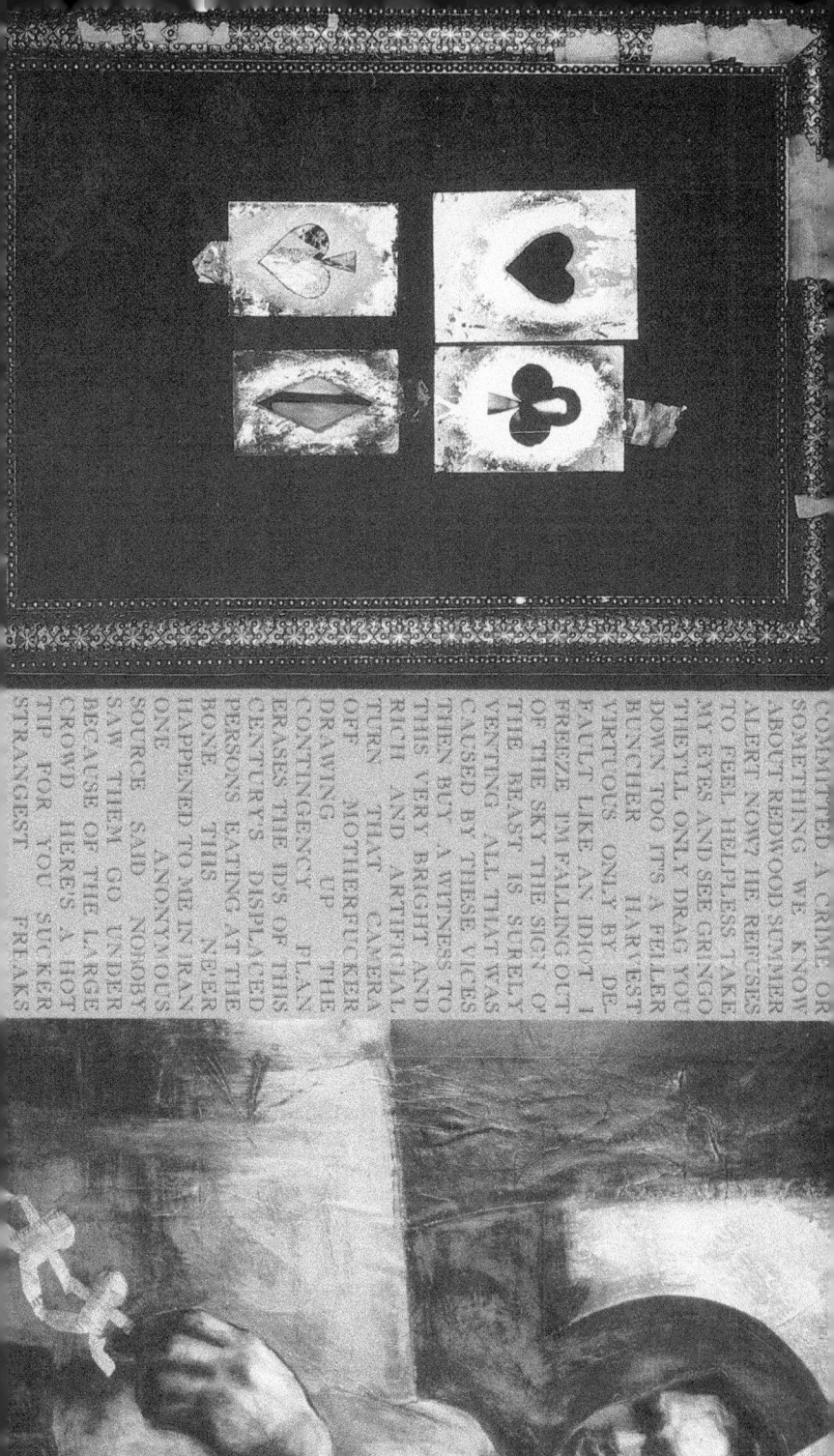

COMMITTED A CRIME OR SOMETHING WE KNOW ABOUT REDWOOD SUMMER ALERT NOW? HE REFUSES TO FEEL HELPLESS TAKE MY EYES AND SEE GRINGO THEY'LL ONLY DRAG YOU DOWN TOO IT'S A FELLER BUNCHER HARVEST VIRTUOUS ONLY BY DE-FAULT LIKE AN IDIOT I FREEZE I'M FALLING OUT OF THE SKY THE SIGN O' THE BEAST IS SURELY VENTING ALL THAT WAS CAUSED BY THESE VICES THEN BUY A WITNESS TO THIS VERY BRIGHT AND RICH AND ARTIFICIAL TURN THAT CAMERA OFF MOTHERFUCKER DRAWING UP THE CONTINGENCY PLAN ERASES THE ID'S OF THIS CENTURY'S DISPLACED PERSONS EATING AT THE BONE THIS NE'ER HAPPENED TO ME IN IRAN ONE ANONYMOUS SOURCE SAID NOBOBY SAW THEM GO UNDER BECAUSE OF THE LARGE CROWD HERE'S A HOT TIP FOR YOU SUCKER STRANGEST FREAKS

Aphasia

Like I see everything
And so it becomes everything I see
It just looks
As far as eyes could see
A look so pure
A pain so pure, so beautiful
A pain so pure, so beautiful
You liar
Hallowed soul
No place to hold
Mass alone
Veils of gold
Eyes of force
Broken form

Shaken clear
Shaken
But it was all it could take

Seldom a sound
Take my eyes and see, gringo
No place to give; no will to live
Five more minutes in denial

Shaken clear
Shaken
But it was all it could take
Take

405

The sign of the beast is surely 405
It was like I committed a crime or something
It's a pattern
I tried to break up with him
He destroyed the paint job on my car
I wake up from a break-in dream and think he's there
The cops can't stop this until he gets serious
If you want a word with him, get in line
Whene'er I see him at work, I shake

And when it took off, I knew it was going down
I opened mine eyes
Still strapped to my seat in waist-deep water
I helped this rescue guy who fainted after the explosion
The few people coming out were blue-skinned from the cold

We are not allowed to give out any information
Her face was frozen, and I knew, and I knew, and I knew
It was like I committed a crime or something
Whenever I see him at work, I shake
I'm sick of being scared all the time
I'm sick of being mad all the time
I'm falling out of the sky

Cobray to the North

Full-auto
Target
The crowd
Down, down
Into the bitter dregs
He refuses to feel helpless

Time for spring cleaning
Time for the street sweeper
Buy the machine designed to clean
thoroughly on the first pass
This blind man just bought a Cobray
M-119

The part that burns me is, the clerk who
sold the gun was an ex-cop
The great humanist only wants to simplify
his life before he dies
I have a corpse in the locked truck in the
back of my head
I met the straw man, who signed Form
4473 for me

It takes greatness like Miami Vice
To increase sales of the Bren 10 assault
rifle
Riding the iron road from Norfolk to the
North
It is the gun that made the '80s roar

1st Wednesday of the Month

Squatting with the sycophant
Reifying the retro-virus
Negating the novenas
Hedging a bet on a heresy
Venting all that was caused by these vices

Between the newborn's first scream and
the newdead's last rattle
Purposely smothering you with
distractions
Perversely feeding on the fly ash

A vile word, a blow
Caught fair in the stomach
To remind him he's still here
Alert now?

They're rearranging the front door
Out the window and down the elm
In Dutch with the neighbors
On the hot seat and freewheelin' the helm

A vile word, a blow
Caught fair in the stomach
To remind him he's still here
Alert now?

And he cannot believe his eyes
As the love of his life sashays into the
bedroom
Arresting with a gesture, she illuminates
and destroys
Those neglected corners where hide his
everyday mockeries

And she cannot believe her ears
As the love of her life expounds from the
bottom of his remaining tarred lung
Tonight, tonight
Multiple incinerators will get it right

Elliot

I remember when he was three
Left the faucet on in the trailer and flooded the whole shebang
It wasn't his fault
Nobody, but nobody should blame him

Too many cigarettes
Too little sleep
I lock myself in the bedroom and cry, cry, cry
It hurts so bad
It hurts so bad that I'm breathless
My guts are pulled in tight
The shame of it all burns, I swear
You can't jump in, said the second-grade teacher
You can't jump in

She was going to be a lawyer
She was going to have twins
She was going to get a convertible so her nappy dreads could blow

You can't jump in

She would gently rock her head against the back of her chair
While she watched horror films
She got good grades, God
God
Nobody saw them go under because of the large crowd
Nobody heard their cries because of the nearby freeway
You can't jump in
It wasn't his fault
Turn that camera off, motherfucker

Too many cigarettes; too little sleep
I lock myself in
I lock myself in
The shame of it all burns, I swear
Th– Thanks
Gimme a chance to catch my breath

Do not attempt to defeat this safety feature of the weak
You can't jump in
They'll only drag you down too

Don't go in the water
Daddy'll be right back
Who would have thought that the neighborhood park could be so dangerous?
They went every week
They went every week
Who'd ever thought this?
Who'd dare think this?
Whenever I close my eyes, I see them in the back seat laughing amongst themselves

I lock myself in
Too many cigarettes
It hurts so bad I'm breathless

Moira Is Vanishing

She always said she was from a trashed family
Once again, her fists crack on my face
A drunken rage that's not about me
This ne'er happened to me in Iran
But I'll stay with her until she falls asleep

One night, both of us in the middle of a bender
I reacted like I was someone else
I know that this is wrong
But it was too much

They came in and didn't even ask me what happened
You Middle Easterners are all the same
Need to be taught a lesson in Western diplomacy
You expect me to believe that a gentle little girl like this could hurt you?
Shut the fuck up, foreigner, and get in

Even if I can't ever get back home, at least I can get away

To the Child Reader

I ask myself, with all these abilities, talent and potential
Why do I hurt, and why am I afraid of me?
I want to get better
My host tells me to trust in these rhymes

Curious beasts of paws and claws
Curious birds of plume and feather
Strangest freaks of nature's laws
Here for ye we bring together

As I'm writing this it's 2/14/83
I suddenly realize my host is sick
High fever, bad cough
I don't know what to do
I'm in love with a man twice my age

Owls and monkeys, pigs and bears
Hummingbirds and toads and rabbits
Hunt them to their nests and lairs
Study all their ways and habits
Learn how the mosquito talks, and why the wasp and hornet sting you
Learn the meaning of the song linnet and

canary sing you
I didn't want to look through your house for paper
So I wrote it all in this book, *The Tao of Physics*
I desperately need the release of

How the beaver builds his dam
How the penguin feeds her babies
Of the lobster and the clam
What their moods and manners may be
All these things, when you shall know
Write a book yourself, my dearie
For so learned you will grow
That all the world will flock to hear ye

This little lamb's a-setting
This little lamb is not
This little lamb's a-fretting
This little Christian's content with her lot
And this is a part of me no one else knows
Save me and you, now

I don't want to die
I want to get better
I don't want to die
I want to live forever

Wordfall

Fall, peacemaker, fall, on the shamrock
My craw freaks as our luck runs dry
To the spin controller's touches
My ruling class's expert psychopath
On a nameless, floating warpath

Leads to the ideal fall
Leads to the ideal fall
Fall
Fall

Buzzbomb free-floating
From meaning to oblivion is rocket, sledding, skidding o'er wordfall
Erases the IDs of this century's displaced persons
Caught in the wrong time
Placed by my psycho euphemistic pariah's nameless cover-up

Fall Fall Fall Fall Fall

Strap me in
I don't have the right words for you
Light the fuse
My words are not your words
Strap me in
I don't have the right words

Fall Fall Fall Fall Fall

Light the true patriot
Light the true patriot
Shoot down these euphemistic strikes

My words
Are not your words
My words
Not your words

My Sister's Living Room

I don't want this lucid dream to ever end
I don't want this lucid dream to ever end
Flying flawless perfect pure
What harm could there be
What harm could there be
What harm could there be in this, in this?

I'm making the devil keep his promise
For a hard-hearted night, I play a counterfeit god
Mere feet above the treeline, I scorch the earth as it falls into my hands

To have a lucid dream look into your hands
When you feel yourself dreaming look into your hands
Start with the plausible before the impossible
No longer weak
No longer vicarious
The only warning, beware the dragon or any other natural anomalies

In my lucid dream, all is calm
From somewhere I can hear the sound of shrieking
I wake up underwater and stupidly take a breath
I stand up and choke up and throw up all over the bathroom
On all fours on the floor
The room spins violently
I try to stand and I get a headrush, and I hear the shrieks again
Get out, get out, get out
I stumble half-naked and dripping into my sister's living room
Well, what would you do?

I can't really tell what's going on upstairs
Like an idiot I freeze
Well, what would you do?

Thinnest Line

Out of the hotel room comes
Yeah, I'll go on a sympathy strike for you
Yeah, I was so patient throughout your greed for jacked synapses
Out of the tower comes crook'd path for a crook'd mile
Logical, always logical smile

One word cut out and repeated endlessly

A jack-in-the-box, the police officer's head bobbed and jerked lopsidedly
I thank God for that painful wisdom
Honestly, now, I've never done this before with sincerity
Without continuity or consequences or mediation sharpened the senses

What is the just price?
What's a happy end?
What sort of complicity are you more comfortable with?

This path, I'm afraid, son, is the most logical

When listening to a song I have never heard
I seem to make up words for it against my will

From time to time when people speak at me
I get the feeling of being o'erloaded

I saw everything very bright and rich and artificial
Like the thinnest line

Looking down on me, he said
This path, son, is the most logical

Stomp

Extractive industries stop at nothing
Driving into the realm of the hungry Holy Ghost
Feeding on aspirations
Vigilantes of the status quo

It's a feller-buncher harvest of ancient knot-free lumber
And any you monkey-wrenchers dumb enough to get in our way
I'm at 18-wheel ramming speed
I'm so close that I can see the little ones in the back seat
The price of my logging job is your life

We know about your plans
We know about Redwood Summer
You can't change the way we live
We are going to show you the stomp

Judi Bari, here is a picture
Your face in a rifle's crosshairs
Come on, baby, do that no-trial boogie
Judi Bari, here is your stomp

Blow, pipe bomb, blow
Drive the nails up through the driver's seat
Into her flesh, into the ceiling
Purify this sick nation of the pagans and the sluts
I am the anointed
I am the hungry Holy Ghost
I am the Lord's Avenger and this is your stomp

Extractive industries stop at nothing
I take credit for the May 24th bombing

Echolocating

It was the start of a perfect friendship
You show me your porta-cell, and I'll show you mine
Quote the pale hypocrite to the smirking ape
Drawing up the contingency plan
Discovered your message on the machine
More of the usual stupid Punch and Judy
Still too cheap to buy yourself one, and the operator so inspired
With my persistence

To your credit, you always suffered
From an ambition
An affliction
An addiction
To goad the subject
Away from the pleasantries
The cotton candy
To the abject witness

Sad to realize how much I depend on you

Been eating at bone
Been eating at me long enough
This is the end of a perfect mistake
You show me your current porta-cell, and I will show you mine
So, my friend, to whome'er hears
If Executive Order 11051 can suspend the glory of America
Then buy a witness to this

Sad to finally realize how much I depended on you

Eidolons

That place that dies
Conscience kills
Beyond the edge and note
The damage pounds
Unknown in water bled red

She said we'd go
It just goes to show
Unbeatable mirth
It just comes and goes

Eidolons possess her

Such reward
This inherent rank of fear at every inch
Flesh to foil
No drop o' sweat could keep a man like you out
A blink of rage in a vile state
I can't remember solitude
The list is dropped and left the photos to the canvases o' your mind

Eidolons possess her, surround her

Overhead it works, but time is hard
Running time may be proportional
Nowhere to hide
It goes on and on
The other side fears the life misplaced
It's not the man that must be protected but the possibilities within him

Eidolons possess her

That place that dies
Conscience kills
Beyond the edge and note
The damage pounds
Unknown in water bled red
She said we'd go

It just goes to show
It just comes and goes
The web of incidence hit her like spikes
With a cool flesh pain, my eyes water
Inside my closet, there lies a pool of mud
It's time to master what you already know

Crawl through my spine, and hold to my light
In sync with my mind
That blows through me, through these walls

Let it in, like a sun
I stand, a post-lintel form of silken life
I am coming home
Home

Eidolons possess her

Slower

One informed source said
This is not enough
This is not enough
I need more
I need
Ravenous, insatiable, voracious
I need more and more and more
More and more and more and more and more and more

One insider source said
Here's a hot tip for you, sucker
Now I'm civilized, so civilized
The lust for expression is placed on the chopping block
The self-enforced repression makes everything deliciously veiled

And then one critic said
Corrupt ways deceived me, and I succumbed to a bloodless indifference
Virtuous only by default, too indolent to be anything at all, at all, at all
Duty, honor, devotion reneged
Duty, honor, devotion reneged

One anonymous source said
I turned away from the herd into the unwelcoming arms of the absurd
One anonymous source said this
Said this
Said this
Said

My will changes like Cleveland's weather
From tea rose and sweat to the ideal's torment
Mania follows repression follows mania follows repression follows mania follows

IX. Zak

CA: That summer [of 1993, after the recording of *craw*], there was a five-week tour we did, where we went out to Minnesota, Seattle. I did that tour. Came back through the Central U.S. We were down in Texas—just a loop. It was a lot of fun. I guess what I'd call it is we were doing a lot of weekend-warrior stuff and maybe taking a week out to play a couple things. Maybe up to Minnesota, Chicago, Kentucky, Pennsylvania, New York. Did we ever get to Boston? I don't remember. Philadelphia. We were doing a lot of those kind of things, and we might have set up two or three nights in a row and sometimes one night there and back. I think all that must've been through '93, but I think we did a lot of that in '92 as well.

Basically, I came out of Case, and I went down to Akron to work on a masters. I'd just gotten married and I was going to have a child. My thinking was, "I'm going to ride this band thing and see where it goes."

They wanted to do a lot more touring; they were saying stuff like, "We need to be on the road 10 months out of the year." It was kind of tough. We were at the craw house, and they sat me down and they're like, "We want to do something more." And I think they knew my situation, where I was and what I was going to say. I was like, "I'm still in school. Gotta pay the bills, guys. If that's what you guys are going to want to do, then I can't do that."

The weekend-warrior thing as we did it, it would've been just fine for me and I was just going to see where it goes and if the whole thing would actually take off. But to not work for 10 months when at that time, craw wasn't making any money... When we did that five-week tour, that was out of our pocket. So that's the story.

RB: So we needed to find a bass player, and if I remember this correctly, a guy who was on and off booking shows for us was from West Virginia, and I don't remember the specifics, but he was like, "There's this kid down in Huntington who's a great bass player; you should meet him."

ZD: I guess the main thing that excited me about [*craw*] was, I have to say at the time, Tool and Helmet were the things I was listening to the most, and both bands are certainly less straightforward than everything that's on the radio but definitely not as interesting as I thought the [first] craw record was. The dynamics of it—there are some pretty good dynamics in Tool, none at all in Helmet, but just the dynamics and the changes and the start-stops. It seemed like [craw's music] was taken so far past the music that I was interested in listening to at the time. It was like the music I was interested in listening to, really expanded upon.

I'd love to remember why I bought it. I think maybe [because] it had that weird, dark album cover with the figure on it. I don't remember. I just remember being at the record store. I might've asked the guy who knew what my tastes were, "What do you have new?" "Check this out." I don't really remember how I got it, but it was just a weird story that I found it in Huntington, WV, and they needed a bass player six months or a year later.

The guy that was booking shows for craw at the time was this guy named Barlow who lived in Huntington. I got in touch with them. I think I talked to Rockie first through Barlow, like, "I hear you need a bass player."

I came up to Cleveland for what was supposed to be an audition, and I was pretty well practiced up. I knew, I don't know how much of the first record, but I knew enough songs that we could jam through them, and get an hour or so of messing around with the music. I couldn't tell you what songs we ended up playing through. We probably picked out the songs [from "craw"] that they would play live the most.

RB: Zak was just finishing up college, or had been in college, and he would come up. He was then still living in Huntington for a number of months. He would come up to try out and we were like, "Yeah, sounds great." I don't remember specifically sitting down with anybody else.

It was like, "Hey, there's this dude. He's really good." "Oh, he wants to do it? Okay, cool—you're in." He would be driving up every weekend to practice, because we had already written most of the material for *Lost Nation Road*, and we had a schedule. We had already booked time with Albini. So it was a crash course for Zak to not only learn the early material, but also to learn the material that we were writing or had written for the second record.

Zak is a phenomenal bass player and musician. If I remember this correctly, he came to some of the first rehearsals or even tryouts and already knew the majority of the first album. Totally prepared, and bringing his talent and musicianship to the band. It was really almost a seamless transition; it was as good as it could have been. And on top of that, his contribution to the material—not only from a riff and creation point of view, but also somebody else came to the table with a riff and basically everyone else would write their own pieces and parts to the riff that was being put out there on the table—his creativeness in that aspect as well was awesome.

DM: After Chris left the band, I don't remember trying out any other bass player besides Zak. If we did, Zak's performance immediately erased that other person's memory. Zak showed up to his "try out" having mastered a huge amount, if not all, of the first craw album. He is a singularly great bass player, and he made a place for himself in the music as a player and a writer.

NC: Chris was a great part of the band. He filled out the bottom in a different way. He was more legato and punkish. Zak, from the get-go, was precisely what the band needed as a bass player as a replacement for Chris. Very different style. I think they also sort of represent the shifts in the band, between the first record and the second record.

Life got too busy for Chris. He couldn't do it anymore. I don't think he wanted to leave the band either; I think he had to make some personal life choices. What I liked about Chris was that he had that punk-rock sound as a bass player, that legato picking kind of thing. But what I really liked about Zak was that the guy already wanted to be in the band before he even joined—you could tell. And then he joined the band and he was great. He really brought a level of technical precision to the bass spot in the group that was something that tightened our sound maybe a little bit. Not only could he play all the previous material; he was a really good part of the new material.

Zak just came in, and he fit immediately, and he got along with everybody and he just worked. He had a great work ethic, and he was really into bass. And he moved to Cleveland from somewhere else to join the band as I recall. Yeah, and a hell of a nice guy; he was just a very amicable person and a supportive player in the group, and he was really excited to be in the group. Zak was just really easy to work with.

Interlude: the craw house

RB: [We practiced] in a little house on the fringes of University Circle and the campus. And at the time, Dave and Joe and a couple of our other friends were living there, so we had the opportunity to rehearse in the basement. Next door to us was another local band, and they rehearsed in their basement as well. But it was just this teeny, teeny little cramped basement, and Dave and Joe were always hitting their heads on the ceiling. It was not spacious by any stretch of the imagination.

DM: The craw house was one of three or four in an isolated row of dilapidated houses on Carnegie Avenue. We shared a steep driveway with the Screwtractor house. Screwtractor was another local band, nice guys with girlfriends who worked as strippers. Carnegie Avenue had four lanes of white-noise traffic whose flow changed from one-way to two-way depending on the time of day, like a tide. Not a residential area. Homeless people would sit on our porch and come in the front door if it was open. Two doors down was a women's health clinic, and for a while, we would be woken every weekend morning by the chanting of anti-abortion protesters with hideously bloody pictures on their signs.

At first it was Joe and I and Tarik [Hussein] living there. Tarik rigged his morning alarm to play the Melvins' *Ozma*, and that woke us on the weekdays. When I moved out to live with my then-girlfriend, another local rocker [Steve Schindler, a.k.a. Ginchy, founder of the band Feeling Crank] moved in and filled what had been my room with broken bicycle parts, floor-to-ceiling and wall-to-wall. He slept on the couch. He was a quirky individual who ruined Joe's tape recorder by trying to record the sound of falling rain, but he was a good guy with a lot of friends. He died somewhat recently of cancer. The craw house and its neighbors have all been torn down, and the empty lots are now planted with grass.

ZD: Joe lived in a house that was referred to as the craw house on Carnegie. It's amazing that it didn't just fall over when we

started playing. It was just the worst house ever, pretty much. A couple other dudes lived there—just a college situation. We practiced in the basement. One of the guys that lived there was into noise, found objects. So he would just bring home all this weird stuff to bang on and make weird creations out of, and he would do little shows like that. So we were crammed into this tiny basement surrounded by the *Sanford and Son* front yard, just garbage everywhere and weird chunks of metal sticking out that could kill you if you slipped and fell.

We practiced a lot—several days a week, usually two or three, and two, three hours at a time, and a Saturday practice that just seemed to last all day. It was serious. We had two fantastic drummers, but the rest of us were barely mediocre players with good ideas. Like, "I have this really great idea, but I can't play it at all, so we're going to have to practice it about 800 times before it'll sound like what I envision it sounding like in my brain."

X. Lost Nation Road

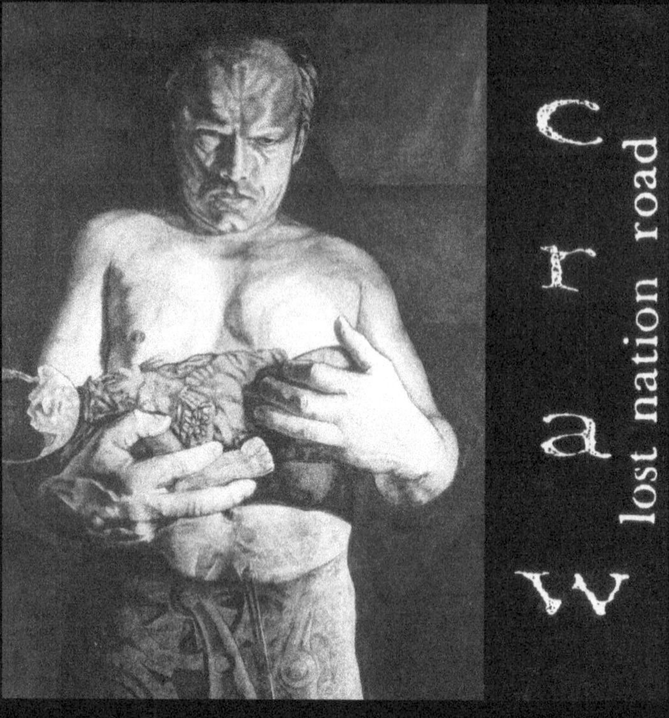

DM: I feel like *Lost Nation Road* is the most old-school record in a way. It's certainly not anything like a concept album, but because the music was written in a tighter time period, because we were all focusing on it, because we were going back to record with Albini and we knew what that would be like, we were able to come up with a bunch of songs that were all conceptualized kind of in the same way. We were able to prepare for the gig a little bit. So I did things like I brought another amp because I knew that it would help me sound the way I wanted to sound.

The records that I like have a specific sonic feeling, and [*Lost Nation Road*] does. The first album was us saying, "This is everything we have; put some mics in front of our amps; capture it as best you can; we're going to play the best we can." And the second one was a little bit more, "Let's make an album." *Lost Nation Road* has an atmosphere.

I think we also had thought about how to tie a few songs together. I think we had thought about it in a way of, if we [tie two songs together], we can maximize it by doing this, like that beginning hit of "Strongest Human Bond."

"Lifelike" was me throwing a whole bunch of stuff into one bag and then at the end of it, Neil having a chance to lay some of his tape music over it. It was me wanting to get specifically "jazzy"-sounding notes in there. And a specific kind of melancholy chordal, harmonic thing that wasn't really in [any other craw song].

To me, the point of the band was, in all ways, trying to transcend all our influences. Take the influences and write stuff that did not sound like anyone else, that did not sound like a specific thing. And when you look at "All This Made Me" or "Sound of Every Promise," those are very bizarre songs that don't sound like other rock songs at the time, or now.

Also the fact that Rockie and I sang on ["Sound of Every Promise"]. He's the first voice you hear. To me, that was a very cool thing, the confidence of, "This first voice you hear is not going to be the lead singer." But at the same time, when Joe steps in, you know that he's the guy. So that inclusivity to me was very cool, and it was a thing that happened throughout the whole record. The saxophones were great, and I think at that point in time, we were pretty open to a lot of stuff.

RB: I don't know if [creating a more cohesive record] was anything that any of us had intended, but I definitely agree [that it is]. The first record was, "Hey, we've got all this shit; we just need to do it"—we had three or four years' worth of material. And the time frame between [*craw* and *Lost Nation Road*] was only a year, so it wasn't intentional; it was probably just natural that it sounded more complete, more focused as a record.

The second record was more evenly broken up between me, Dave and Neil. Neil actually composed a number of the songs from a drum perspective, and then whatever instrument we were playing, we would try to find things that fit. So "Botulism, Cholera and Tarik" was Neil's, and "All This Has Made Me." There was definitely more of a creative evenness in terms of specific people bringing stuff to the table.

ZD: The only song on *Lost Nation Road* that I wrote was "Feesh Crik." I had written that previously. The intro to that was something that Rockie wrote. We were on tour and soundchecking or warming up before a show, and I was like, "Oh, I've got this song that I had written before I was in craw." And Rockie had that intro and he was going to put it into something else, and was like, "Oh, I've got this intro." We kind of sandwiched them together and that became "Feesh Crik."

DM: Albini was kind of peaking in a way—his publicity was peaking. The first album was before he did Nirvana, and the second album was right after. At the beginning, I think he had just moved into the house. He was unsure about his relationships with his neighbors; I think he had more starting-up-a-new-business worries. And the second one, the phone wouldn't stop ringing. There was a lot of controversy about his [Nirvana] mixes.

For us, it was rock-star heaven. The Frogs came into the studio and chatted with Albini. And someone else came in, and [Steve] said, "Oh, you can borrow whatever," and he said, "Oh, that was so-and-so from Slint." It was super cool. Nobody was exploding with glee; it just was happening right in front of your face, and the stuff sounded great. And of course, he's Albini, so he says, "Where do you want this tape splice?" We learned a lot.

ZD: We recorded music [for *Lost Nation Road*] first, and the set-up in Albini's basement at the time was, you came down the stairs and there was sort of a bigger room that was more open, it seemed, where the drums set up, and then there was a door. The house is sort of long and narrow, so the drums were set up looking at the door to the next room, which was a more sound-proofed, smaller but longer room. And we were in there with our amplifiers, sort of lined up, each looking over the other's shoulder trying to see Neil for visual cues. So it was not the most conducive playing situation for sure. I'm sure we had to Septarate the drums and guitars, but it was a challenge. And if I recall, I was all the way at the back. Probably putting the bass player furthest away from the drummer isn't going to help things out too much. So I was clear in the back of this room, probably 15 or 20 feet away from Neil, looking at him through a little doorway.

It was all live. Albini was Albini, so he was really against overdubbing guitars and stuff like that. And if we got through 90 percent of the song and effed up the last bar, we would record that and Albini would actually splice tape, which is mind-boggling that he could do that and just have it turn out seamless.

Mixing was exciting because it's a million-year-old board, and the whole band would be up on the faders having to orchestrate. Rockie would be a little louder on this part, so Rockie would actually have to be up on his faders a little bit and then it gets quiet here and the bass gets a little loud, so I'd actually have to ride my fader. So if you can imagine three or four of us all standing at the mixing board doing a little dance to try to get it to sound out, which I believe Albini sort of facilitated that. Of course everybody wants their part to be louder than everything else, so probably Albini had to go back when we weren't looking and make changes. I can't say that happened for a fact, but...

RB: What I do remember that was really more interesting this time around was that Joe was more interested in getting weird tonal sounds out of natural devices or mechanisms. And Steve was really into that. So on some of the tracks, Joe would have a microphone on the other side of the room, and in between that microphone and himself, Steve would have a microphone hanging from the ceiling, spinning [in a circle], so it would catch things stronger on the one side and float off on the other side as it was spinning around, making all these really creative and unique vocal sounds. I remember those guys spending a bunch of time on that, which was really kind of fun to watch.

Joe was like, "Let's do some really cool stuff, and I don't want it to be electronically modified in the studio. I want the stuff to be natural." I don't know where he got some of these things, but he had this tube with these big springs on it, on the outside of this metal tube. Steve may have had the microphone on the other end of this tube. But as he sang through it, the springs would actually vibrate and hit the tube, so there was this weird metallic echo to everything Joe was singing through it. So that was kind of cool.

ZD: I do remember going down and watching Joe, and I know he did a lot stuff handheld, and he did a lot of stuff holding his various weird implements up to the microphone. I just remember going down one time and seeing him totally crouched over like he'd be at a live show, holding the microphone.

I remember he had a tube; he just found this very thin steel tube that had three or four springs on it. He sang into one end and held the microphone up to the other end. And I think they put a contact microphone on the bottom of the snare drum head, and he actually had his lips touching the top snare drum head and sang through that. On some songs, you can hear the snares rattle.

DM: Joe brought two milk cartons full of stuff, like what you might want to call analog effects. Him singing through a snare drum. Albini used this mic technique that I now think he got from Bowie, because I hear some of it on *Scary Monsters*, where there's a vocal mic here, but there's a vocal mic over there [across the room]. So if you start raging out, when you hit a certain volume, that vocal mic in the corner is going to pick up and it's going to pick up the room around you, so you go from this close-up feeling to all of a sudden, a guy screaming in a big room and then it comes back.

JM: I started with [an] effects rig early on [in the band's history]. At the time I was enamored with adding more noise to the vocals, to further de-emphasize the importance of the vocals. Later, effects on the albums were simply done because I like the effect. I got the "singing through a snare drum" shtick after watching Neil holler through his snare.

NC: Both Matt Dufresne and Marcus DeGrazia had become immediate good friends of mine when I met them in Ann Arbor at University of Michigan, and we started jamming together up in Ann Arbor, in different configurations of musicians that were at school at UMich. We were listening to jazz together; we were turning each other on. Matt, I think he was the first person I ever listened to *A Love Supreme* with; that's pretty fuckin' huge. He became one of my best friends. So those guys became hangin' buddies with me, and we used to play this really avant-ish improv and sometimes arranged jazz stuff. I was very influenced by the Knitting Factory recordings, and what was going on in New York at the time. We were all really into John Zorn and a lot of the other edgy approaches to jazz: Elliott Sharp and Carbon, Fred Frith.

And so, yeah, wanting to get them involved in craw was like, "Hell yeah, let's do this." By the time we were recording the second record, number one, they were two very, very close friends of mine and also they had become friends with everyone in craw, and they were big fans of the band. So it was kind of a no-brainer for those guys to do it. And I wanted to include things that were outside of what people were used to sonically; I loved the sound of the growling, flipping-out saxophone—reed-biting, throat harmonics. So yeah, it was just trying to expand what we were doing, fuck with people's perceptions of what we were or what we could be and just keep pushing that envelope.

RB: I know we did a number of shows locally before we headed off to record that record with [Matt and Marcus] onstage with us, and it was chaotic and crazy and beautiful. I love the way it came out. It was complete improv to a degree, especially at the end of "Botulism." I remember we were down there while they were doing this, and they were like, "Should we stop?" And Neil's sitting there on the stairs like, "Keep going!"

Sound of Every Promise

She looked it in the eye
I've got an empty
I don't have any more dreams
I wrote a letter
Then I buried it
Everything's exposed in the dark
Empty closet, empty shelves
No waking moment has ever touched this
I need a fear all my own
Widening the cracks that run through my wall
Nothing left to touch save the grains on the sill
I can't fill the closet
I can't fill the shelves
Just want to taste your presence
An empty vial, a hand-made book, velvet shoes
(Breathe, breathe)
The healing touch fades
I've got an empty
I've got an empty
Nothing survives the cracked shell of time
Time

Opened my eyes to no name and white memory
Her voice the voice of heroines in my sleep
I couldn't tell where the stories left off
And my dreams began
(Time, time, time)
As I closed my fingers the world I touched turned to sand
She glimmered like the ice, floating away from me, on the water
Deathless, the hard white of that scar

Woke to the black roar of trains passing through blurred towns
(Breathe, breathe, why won't you breathe?
Breathe, breathe)

Through the camera before the roar
Right before the stick hit
She looked across the crowd
And she told him that she loved him
The blow shattered her skull
I don't miss the past anymore
And the music was gone

Strongest Human Bond

Six years later my twin was born
Bearing all that is me

Same royal stain
On the upper torso
Predisposed to bottom feeding

His sole deviation
Was a predilection
For making the flames dance

Carelessly
As he said, "I swore I put it out. I swore I saw it fade out."

And I watched the flames rise higher than the elm
And I waited
And I watched the flames fade out
He was the only one

After that carny of reason
Every midwinter was the same
Fading
Sinking
Fading
Sinking
I always enjoyed that sinking
Fading
Sinking

Twenty years later my twin is passed out on the couch
He is past my regard
A solicitor man done told me
That the strongest human bond
Is that of twins
So that if one is accidentally maimed
The other will be all the more compensated
Struck a match
Put it out
Stuck another
And I waited
I waited

Bypass

The grandkids ask her questions
That she can't or won't ever answer
This is the inheritance
That will never be passed down
Over and over, she tells her son, "They
all know.
They all know. They're all staring at me."
Had to come to Cleveland
For her husband's bypass
Met a white kid in a mall
Who said, "How did you know I was one?"

"You remind me of someone I once knew
Twenty years ago, back in Indian school."

Been fifteen years since I've seen your
red eyes.
Just wanted to see the grandkids one last
time
I dream in fire
A blaze that brings me here
Don't know if I know you
Don't know if I care

Bury the world for me
I hold myself before it all

Somewhere in Southern South Dakota
Just off I-90
A place I've only heard about or seen in
snapshots
A transplanted cabin stands
Speaks of her and Ducharme
And when we finally go
It'll be as foreign for me
As it will be for you

Botulism, Cholera, and Tarik

Somehow there's this old man, all hair and nails, making all this racket, that I decipher in a clear globe that I spy inside my mattress. Glass monkey's so afraid. He bashes to and fro. He bloodies his nose and he quits.

A sudden pounding on my bedroom door redirects my last eye. A repairman reaches into the mattress, screws in a new old man, saying, "They have a tendency to burn out after a while."

I freak for a second, and then I am fine.

Lifelike

Over the net
Before it got erased
I read this mash note
To life's undying lash:

We'll invent a more glorious accident. We will bend time with the speed of our weapons. We will pervert the meaning of the word civilian. No time for reflection, no means of deterrence, no need for holding camps. We will simply make them disappear.

Come join the evacuation march
From city to suburb
In the name of security,
In the name of speed
Everything deregulated, disintegrated
We end up defeated,
Without there ever having been a war

Took the MLK off the lakeshore freeway
The locals set up the customary trap for
a carjack
Took a one way going the wrong way
And when I got home I just sat there
And waited
For all of it to stop continuously replaying

Pure speed
Pure war
Pure speed
Pure war

We'll continuously colonize our own cities

Behind the wheel
It's a sensation like I'm staring at the T.V.
And anything I decided to ram
I would simply pass through
I've become
Pure speed
Pure war
Pure speed
Pure war
Pure speed

I Fought Dirty

When I walked
I walked as any other
Man
And when I chose to discourse
It was as any other
And when I fought
I fought as dirty as any other
Only the crone could discern what I had discovered
And she laughs
At my small town indiscretion
Crone claws for my ears
Cackles about the bloodletting
"Boy, take a hard look at yourself
in my funhouse mirror.

Let's review the crime you say you sired.

Where's your accomplice?
Where's your instrument?
Where's the body?"

Crone midwife murmurs,
"Here's the knife.
Cut it,
Cut the cord."

I can still see her amid the shiny floors
White starched uniforms
And the stink of day-old urine

Articles on the wall, ignored
Cut the cord

All This Has Made Me

It's a column of water
As tall as the World Trade Center
Shot at heaven
At a rate of
Two hundred miles per hour
White foam circle
At surface zero
Boiling everything for two miles around

Years before, towed two boatloads
Full of friends and companions beyond recognition
Out to the open sea to be sunk

He hands me two bottles of bourbon
And says,
"Go to the officer's club and drink it off."

Every day for what would end up to be
The longest tow in naval history
I stare back at the mangled disabled ship
And think how obsolete
All this has made me

We watched the film clips
All the top brass were there

Days later, fell apart
Rested for six months
Wouldn't accept a pysch disability
Worked a couple of more months until I retired

Disclassified I
Will speak my peace
Towering wall of water
Racing at my ship
Bouncing two feet off the ocean
The screaming and drifting
Toward
Surface zero
Six thousand men
Left holding the bag

Shocklight

Such a willing slave was I
Catering to the most immaterial disloca-
tions
Listen to this organ grinder
Lay waste to liver and kidney

Set the selector for the visceral devices
A soft word
Insistent pressure
Peach juice on lips
The trace scent of gardenias
The brilliance of the sun
Exploding over Lake Erie

God, I-80 was boring
Obscene,
Nothing to see
Like her verbal shocklights
Abstractions no longer for me

In the Greyhound mental lockdown
In a position of sleeplessness

Diesel fumes
Snow blindness
The remnants
Of her shocklights

Wise guy that he was
He just made it all the worse

Traveling far and away from the
Flameout wreckage of his severing

On an abandoned railroad trestle
He starts a prolonged disfiguring

He, so depraved
She, so unscathed
When he felt stong enough
He burns the lovelock

The give-and-take deteriorating
Into a confused and crawling need
And he shouts down his nightly insomnia
With this one thought
There's nothing
So disgusting
As a willing
Slave

Feesh Crik

Parched, parched, parched
You may be uncomfortable
Don't be concerned about it
Some swelling may occur
After it all wears off
The extraction may bleed
For a couple of hours
O ye of ricochet type
Reduced to reptilian
To help control bleeding
Follow this procedure
Go back into the quarry
Next to which the feesh crick is running
dry
Let the arid heat cook your skull
As fever delusions become solutions
Forcing identity complete with pseudonym
To fill the extraction
Something to hide behind
Coward
Don't be fooled into actually
Taking a stand
Let's play the name game
Just call me
The Feesh Crik Kid
Shedding five years
In a weightless moment
And another thing
Who let the killjoy in here
Who let laughing boy in here

They say snake people are special
They can take the bite
Transmutate poison into blood

As Long as the Turnpike

Greetings
From the third most toxic state
In the grand ol' U.S.A.

Dear sir,
The above creditor has referred their
claim against you to this office. We are
authorized to take action necessary to
secure final determination of your debt.
Failure to respond will result in you being
held accountable for the consequence of
your neglect.

Go ahead
If you're to be my accountant
All those times I've mistaken your best
intention
Go ahead
Promise what you can never deliver

You and I repeatedly have conversation
So toxic
So false
Its waste should be shot
In those deep injection wells
Located outside of Fremont

Go ahead
Stuff your sad little tale into the autoclave

You and I repeatedly have conversation
So toxic
So false
Its waste should be destroyed
In the world's largest burner
Soon to be built on the banks
Of the Ohio

The last time you whistled in from out
of state
Hauling medical waste
And misdirected grudge
As long as the turnpike
This time I wash my hands of it all

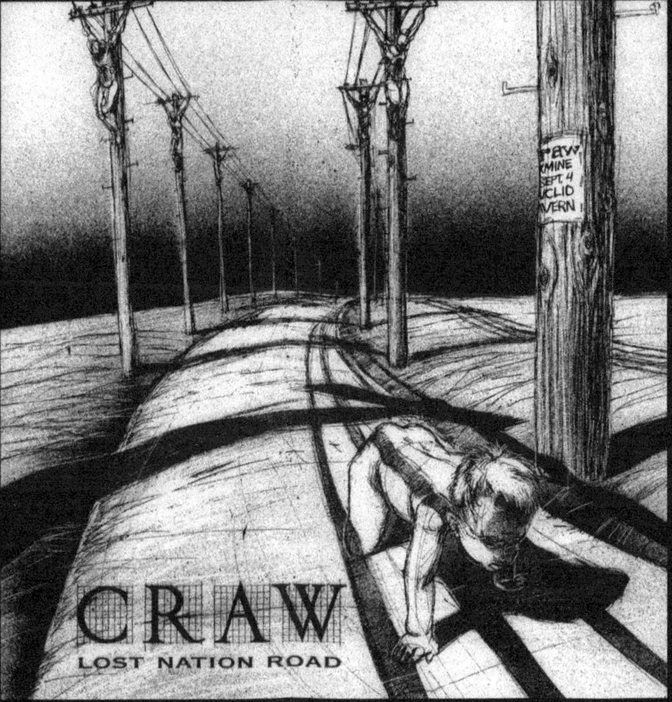

CRAW
LOST NATION ROAD

XI. Will

NC: What happened with me in '95 is that I got an interview with the city of Cleveland Department of Recreation to teach drums and music at a variety of rec centers. It was a part-time job, but one that would pay my bills, and I [could] focus on music. And craw had already booked an eight-week tour with Glazed Baby—that monster tour that I wish I would've gone on still, in some ways. But I had to choose between one or the other, and I guess I just decided at that point that I was going to have to move on. That was a tough decision to make.

WS: I got a call from Rockie that things were dicey with Neil, and Rockie wanted to know if I would be interested in playing with the band. And I was like, "Are you fuckin' shitting me, dude?" I used to go to craw shows all the time and just crack up because the arrangements are so ridiculous. There's five people there; I'm one of the only people that are watching this band, but holy fucking crap, that band rocked. In the most ridiculous way, which I found pretty endearing. I used to watch craw and just drool and giggle like a little kid.

RB: I did this side project called 10 Tons of Hell, and Will was drumming, and that's when I was like, "Damn, that dude's crazy and really talented in a really bizarre way." So I had actually been working with him on and off right around that time when Neil left. So I immediately asked him, and he was like, "Sure, okay."

It was funny, Bill Korecky [friend of the band, and engineer on various craw recordings], when he heard that Will was going to be drumming for us, he said, "What the hell are they thinking? They can't do that!" And then when we went and recorded *Map, Monitor, Surge,* Korecky was just like, "Holy shit—I never knew how good he was!"

[Will] did his best to mimic a lot of what Neil was doing, but Neil is so closed and tight and precise, and Will is so open and bashing and bizarre. It was a huge change that especially me and Zak from that core rhythm section really needed time to get used to.

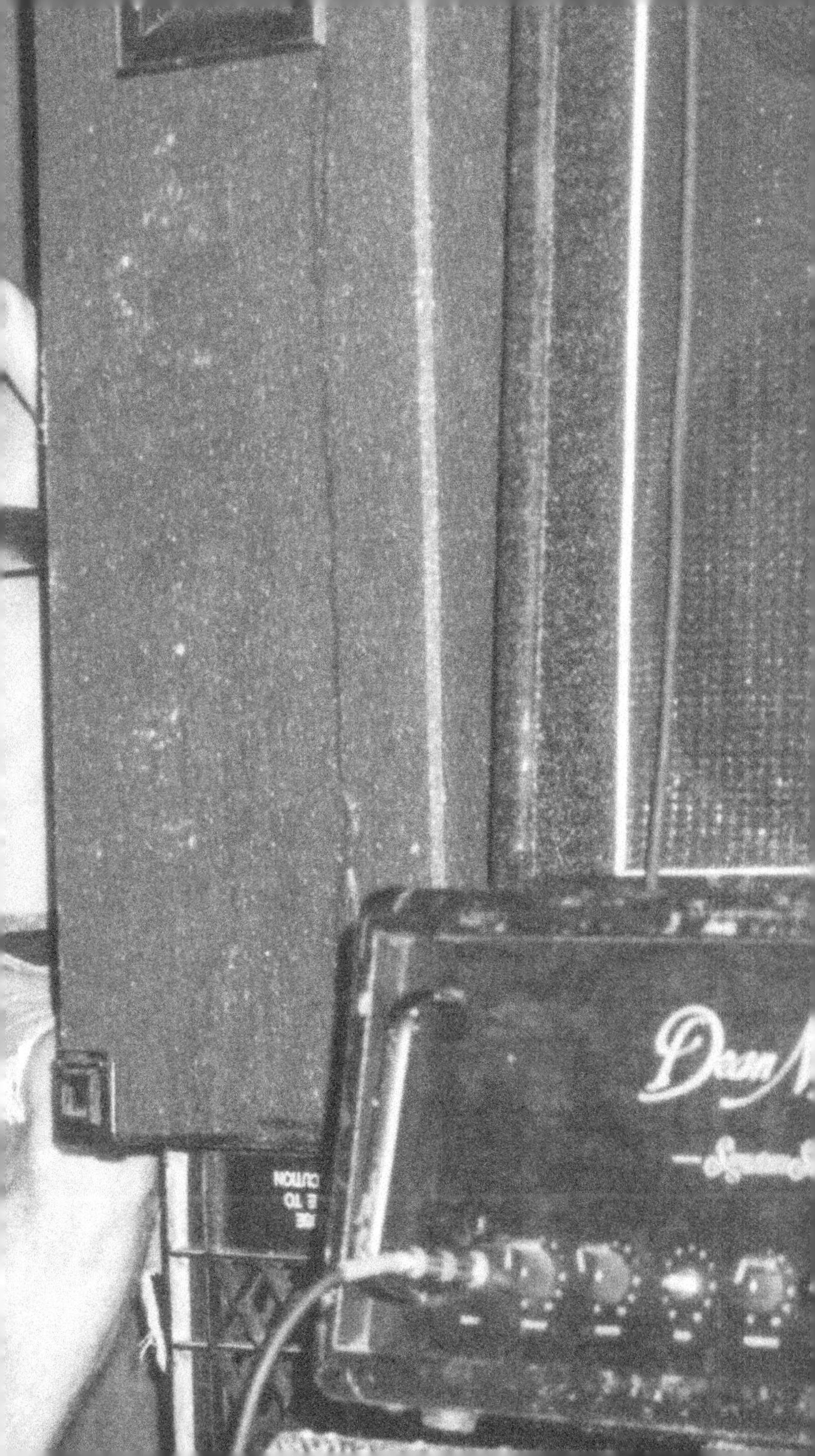

ZD: I knew Will just very briefly before this. Rockie was pretty good friends with him. He was in this band called 10 Tons of Hell, which was a three-piece. Frank Cavanaugh, who eventually ended up in Filter, was the bass player, and they were a really good just kind of dirty rock band.

So I went to see them play once, and Will's got no shirt on, and this is back in the day when he was a bodybuilder dude, and he's all ripped and he's beating the hell out of his drum set, and he'd hit one crash cymbal and it would fall over, so he'd be playing with one hand and reach over and pick up the crash cymbal with his other hand. And he'd reach over and hit his hi-hat and he'd do the same thing. This drum set was just falling apart all around him.

DM: When he started with us, his shit would just fly away from him and we would just laugh. It literally seemed like his drums were like, "Stop hitting me!" They were just running away from him in terror. And he probably still does this; he would nail the kick drum to the stage. He used to have a chain that would wrap around his stool to the hi-hat to the kick drum.

ZD: So we're having a post-Neil band meeting, "What are we going to do?" And Rockie was like, "I'm pretty good friends with this Will guy. He loves our band, so he'd love to be in it." And I was like, "You mean that guy from 10 Tons of Hell? You've got to be fucking kidding me. They're a great band, but there's no way that idiot's going to be able to play craw music." I was pretty adamant about it: "We'll try it out, but I can't see it ever working out." So we had a practice. There was a school over in the hood that was converted into apartments and rock-band practice spaces, so that was where Will was set up. We moved all our crap over there and did a practice with him, and it was kind of like one of those "And the rest is history..." moments.

The minute we played together, I was totally relieved. There was an immediate connection, and I was impressed that he was not interested in filling Neil's shoes, but in staying true to his own style and instincts. Craw just instantly became a very different band.

WS: Zak's really easy to lock in with; I'm sure he's easier to lock in with than I am, by a long shot. He's a great player; he's super percussive, and he knows where to put the dead notes and the spaces, and all of that stuff. He's badass. He's super easy to play with, and he's really big on listening to the other guys, paying attention to dynamics. He's a real communicative player.

DM: It was a certain band with Neil that was very polished and tight and a certain amount of anxiety about being polished, and then with Will, it was kind of like, we're a fierce band that is occasionally very messy, but we're still very fierce and the songs are very fierce, and when we hit it, when we actually it get it all together, it might even be more aggressive.

RB: The Neil craw and Will craw have two drastically different feels to them, but are both pure and absolute craw.

WS: [Neil and I] are completely different players. I hear the riff and I play along with the riff, and Neil knows exactly what the riff is; he knows all the ins and outs and the numbers and how to count it. I hear a riff, and I play it. I have no idea what it is; I don't really know what the time signature is; I just can feel it, so I know where the 1 is. I think I tend to dance around that stuff more, like play around the 1 as opposed to hitting the 1 every time, and that's probably the big difference in our playing. He's more literate and direct, and I don't have a clue how to read music.

With craw, you've got to write that stuff down when you're first learning it, because there's so many weird numbers. Most rock music only has anywhere from two to four riffs in a song. But the craw songs, there would be ten, sometimes 12 riffs in a song. There's a shitload of riffs in these songs. Or there's a riff that keeps getting added to, and it's one note, so it changes the meter all up. So anyway, the cheat sheet would be, like, "A, three times; B, two times; C, five times," and a note about each transition in there somewhere. But it was, you know, caveman-style, written on magic marker on a notebook. You take the page and you put it next to the drums and poof, you know? There were a couple songs where I still had to keep the notes onstage halfway into a tour to make sure I didn't fuck something up. There was one song—I think it was a song on *Map, Monitor, Surge*. There was a spot where the counts are, like, 4, 3, 2, 5, 4, 3, 5, 2—whatever. I forget the numbers, but I had that written on my snare drum head all the time, because I had to refer to it. I think I did that for, like, three tours, till I finally had it in my head, and I could do it without looking at the cheat sheet.

[Craw songs were] either Rockie's song, Zak's song or Dave's song. It wasn't like, "Okay, I've got these riffs and we've got to figure out a way to put them together—anybody got any ideas?" It was like, "Okay, here's the song." They'd come to practice with a song and play the song first, maybe once or twice all the way through, so we'd get a road map of where it goes. And then we'd start breaking it down, dissecting it into riffs. And that's pretty much what you have to do; you have to do it riff by riff and part by part, and experiment with what to play over the riff. And that's one thing I like to do, is play the thing over and over again, play one riff for ten minutes and just jam over that riff, and I'll listen to it later and pick out what drum part I like best. I'll try out 25 different drum parts for a riff, and I'll listen to it and be like, "That drum part's cool; I like that. So I'll use that for this riff." Or, "I really like these three, so I'll play this part for the first time the riff comes around; then the next time the riff comes around, I'll play it this way; then I'll play it this way."

The band was pretty gung-ho about biting off new material. That was one thing about craw that was awesome. As opposed to a lot of other bands, nobody wants to really dig in and conquer the hard stuff; they want the stuff that's easy, the low-hanging fruit. But craw was a band that was not afraid to do completely ridiculous stuff and obsess over five seconds' worth of music for a whole practice. That was one of the first things I thought: "Man, they must spend so much time practicing one little segment. How do they do this?" Because I was awestruck, listening to the records [before I was in the band]. That's pretty much how we did it—just spending a lot of time. That was in the nature of the band, just like, "Okay, got to get it right."

Joe wasn't a singer at all. He was just a guy that got thrust into a band, and I think that's one of his greatest strengths. He wasn't playing by the rules of vocal tradition. He was just doing what he did. So it made him sound a really disturbed, messed-up, tormented individual telling a story about this crazy thing that happened in his life. If you listen to it, it's like, "Wow, whose life is that? It's not a life I want to be living." Or maybe, "It is a life I want to be living," depending on the song. He was a storyteller, man. He wasn't really a singer or vocalist. He was kind of another instrument in the band as opposed to being a vocalist or a frontman, or whatever, which I always thought was pretty cool.

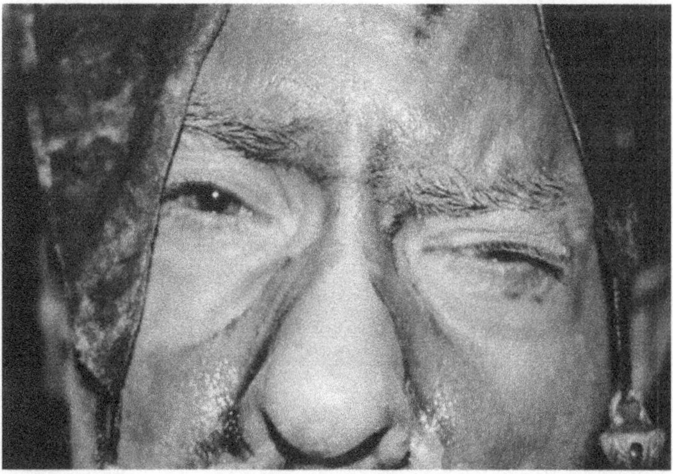

XII. Tour

RB: From the time that that first record came out, really the only places that [craw] was received well were regionally around Cleveland, so Akron, Columbus, Pittsburgh, Youngstown, Buffalo to a certain degree. As we put out more records and logged more time on the road, New York was always great, Boston was always great. We always had a great turnout in a lot of the Jersey cities. Kansas City. Chicago was always really good because that's where [Choke, Inc.] was for those two records. So that would constitute the core of the cities that really came out and really enjoyed the band.

There were also those weird one-offs—"Holy smokes, where did this come from?" We had some friends down in Mississippi, and we ended up playing some show in Panama City, Florida, and all these people who were fans of the band in Mississippi and Alabama caught wind that we were actually going to be kind of close, and [they] all came down and it was a really great show.

ZD: Boston and Kansas City were always very well received, and everywhere else, not so much. And places where we thought we should've been good at... It all makes sense to me now, but at the time, we had this vision of ourselves as being the next Jesus Lizard. We really wanted to be a hipster indie-rock band, and so we played these shows in Chicago and New York where we just thought, "They're gonna think we're awesome." We were definitely more metal than we thought we were, and as soon as Rockie would chunk away on some Metallica riff during soundcheck, all the hipsters would just walk out. And at the end of the show, there would be, like, three guys down front, little 16-year-old hardcore kids that thought it was awesome.

DM: Chicago, I feel like they were too smart for us, and too together. Their scene was way more fully formed than anything that had really happened in Cleveland. So they looked at us, a band from Cleveland, like we just burrowed out of a tree. We would play with people from Chicago and it just would not land.

FORD
GRUMPY

TAR
DAZZLINGKILLMEN
AAA Plus
52000 REWARD

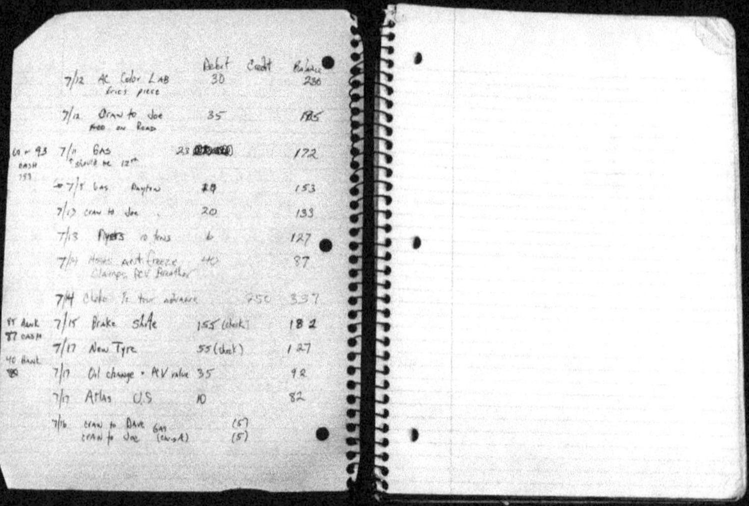
Debit Credit Balance
7/12 AC Color LAB 30 230
Eric's piece
7/12 Drawn to Joe 35 195
Food on Road
7/11 Gas 23 172
should be 12th
7/13 Drawn to Joe 20 133
7/13 Flyers 10 tens 6 127
7/14 Hoses anti freeze Clamps PCV Breather 40 87
7/14 Check ½ tour advance 250 337
7/15 Brake Shite 155 (check) 182
7/17 New Tyre 55 (check) 127
7/17 Oil change + PCV valve 35 92
7/17 Atlas U.S 10 82
7/16 Drawn to Dave Gas (5)
Drawn to Joe (Chris A) (5)

CRAW
AND
GLAZED BABY
YOU GUYS PLAY LIKE A BUNCH OF GIRLS TOUR '95

SEASON TO RISK
craw
TOUR 1997

SOUND OF --
CANCER
BOTULISM
COBRAY
STRONGEST
FEESH CRIK
405
ALL THIS
LIFELIKE

Sound
Cancer
Botulism
COBRAY
Strongest
Feesh Crik
405
Lifelike
ALL THIS

WILL NITRO
N. CAROLINA

DIVINITY
SHORTIE
TRICKIE
DUBBIE
BUTTERFLIES

CANCER MAN

ZD: We played some basement shows, little punk-rock basement shows with local hardcore bands—and I have no idea how we got on these shows—that were the best shows ever. We were just aiming our music at the wrong crowd, for sure. Like, 25-year-old hipsters were not going to like craw, but 15- or 16-year-old hardcore-punk kids would. And we didn't really see that, unfortunately. That didn't become clear to us until much, much later.

There were definitely bands, like the Dazzling Killmen or Today Is the Day, that made more sense to play with them than a lot of what was out there. But it was a lot of just playing with the local band that sounded like Helmet. It was amazing—every night we'd play with a band of 16-year-old kids that sounded exactly like Helmet, again and again. And every once in a while, you'd come across some band that was just weird. Down in Florida, we played with this band called Knucklefish that was really good and just weird. They had heard of us, and they were like, "We heard you were coming down, so we got on the bill to play because we like you guys." Little things like that happened.

DM: It's hard to overstate how bad our luck was with [touring]. One that really sticks out was, we were somewhere in Kansas and we came up to this place, and it was a roadside shack. It's a single building in a parking lot. We pull up and we talk to the guy, and it's Tuesday night and it's the pool tournament night. So we're saying, "All these people are here to play pool against each other. No one here wants to hear us." We were trying to tell the bartender or owner or the booker, and he just didn't care. He said, "If you want to get paid, you have to play." And we were playing at that point for probably 60 bucks. So Will and I got up onstage and just improvised whatever. I think we played "Immigrant Song," and I played and sang. We played a bunch of stuff. And at the end of it, some woman comes running out of the crowd and grabs me and gives me a big smooch, because they're all drunk as coyotes. We got our 60 bucks, and we filled up the tank and we left.

Then finally you would start to meet these other bands: La Gritona, Dazzling Killmen, Glazed Baby, Season to Risk. Meeting those guys was definitely, like, "Okay, things aren't any better out here on the road, but this is lifting our spirits and these guys have been doing this as long as we have, and they know the ropes." It made going to the Waffle House every day and eating grits more entertaining.

DARIN GRAY (DAZZLING KILLMEN): I don't remember how Dazzling Killmen and craw began with each other. But I think it was probably through Nick [Sakes, Dazzling Killmen guitarist-vocalist], who had some type of connection with one of them, and I do know that we drove specifically all the way to Cleveland to play a show with them at the Euclid Tavern. So we drove up there, and we had never heard them, because of course, at the time, there was no way to hear them. It was before their first record came out. We played and then they played, and when they played, I honestly will never forget that. I've played thousands of shows now, and it's etched in my memory. I was completely blown away. And also, I had this overwhelming feeling of not being alone anymore. Dazzling Killmen, we always felt alone. And it wasn't just that we were thinking, "Oh, we're so unique; we're so original." It was more like, we were from a small city [St. Louis]. No one here really cared what we were doing. When we would play out of town, the response was not great, at least at that time. And hearing craw really made me feel less alone and made all of us feel less alone.

And also, I think probably at the time, live, that was the most unique band I had ever heard. There really isn't another band like craw. They're a completely unique entity. And I remember just thinking, like, "Wow, someone has worked as hard as we have on a completely different thing." It wasn't that craw sounded anything like Dazzling Killmen, and quite the contrary, really nothing like it. I could tell, I could hear that they had honed it and worked on it to the highest level. And at the time, there weren't a whole lot of bands out there touring that were like that, that had honed something to that high of a level.

Also, the only reason I felt that they did hone their craft the way they did was because they felt they had to; they felt compelled to be great, to be the best they could be. And for no other reason. There was no gain; there was absolutely nothing to gain, and I could tell they knew that. Because we were playing that first show with them in Cleveland, and honestly, my guess would be there were 25 people there, maybe 30.

From there, we would stay with them when we played there. We played there as much as we could, and in fact, we loved craw so much that we would drive from St. Louis to Cleveland with no other shows and drive back. I remember even driving up, playing the show and driving back the same night, because people had to be at work the same day. We loved them; we literally loved them. And all of those guys were just the absolute most golden guys on earth. Then we started sharing shows. They would come down to St. Louis and play—maybe three times, maybe four—shows that we would set up for them down here, and they would open for us. The response here was probably the response they got everywhere, just people being perplexed. Even with their own crowd and even in their own town, people were pretty perplexed, man, you know? For me, honestly, I was not perplexed by what they were doing.

[Dazzling Killmen and craw were] a genre of two of bands that do not sound alike, that maybe at the core figured out a way to be heavy, if you will, without the baggage of genre.

RB: The [Glazed Baby and Season to Risk tours, in 1995 and 1997, respectively] were the longest. A lot of the cities, you're playing to 20 people, and a handful of them are actually there to see you. You're making gas money and eating pizza and sleeping on people's floors.

[The Glazed Baby tour] was a fun tour. Those guys were crazy. Joel [Hamilton, guitarist] had this video camera, and he was videotaping everything. The Season to Risk guys were awesome. We were coming from Providence going to NYC, and we were both touring in these big white-whale vans with the extended back and camper top, and we were driving down the highway next to each other, and they opened up their side door and just started hurling fruit. We had stopped off at some farmer's market and gotten these big crates of fruit. So it was a fruit war at 80 miles an hour with these two huge white vans.

WS: We were on tour probably four months out of the year, but not making any money, so we were spending eight months trying to dig ourselves out from this snowstorm of bills. And right about the time you got your life back to normal, you were on the road again.

ZD: Has anybody ever told you the "getting pulled over in Texas" story? We're coming back from SXSW or somewhere in Texas. On the way down, Joe got drunk and Dave convinced him that he always wanted to be in a band with a singer with a mohawk, so Joe ended up getting a mohawk. And another time, Joe was drunk and passed out and somebody decided to write in a magic marker across his chest "I smoke pot." So those were the two things leading up to this.

So we're driving in Texas; it's about a million degrees. I think this must've been back in the Neil days because it was our old green van that had the floor of it rusting out. So Joe had no shirt on, with "I smoke pot" written across his chest, a mohawk and he had taken one of his shoes off because it was hot in the van, and he had his left foot up in the little step-up place in the van that was all rusted out, to be air-conditioned, and his other shoe on, on the gas pedal. And we got pulled over, and the Texas cop asks him, "Step out of the van." And we're just like, "Oh, this is not gonna go good at all."

So he's standing there in front of a Texas cop with "I smoke pot" written across his chest and a mohawk and one shoe off and no shirt. And we mentioned that we were just at SXSW and the cop goes, "Oh, really? You guys know the Butthole Surfers?" We're like, "Yeah." He's like, "Oh, I know somebody from that band! Okay, keep it under 90—see you later!" And we got back in the van and drove away. That's one of our good-luck moments.

Interlude: Cambodia Recordings

ZD: I don't know exactly when [Choke, Inc.] came apart, but [the label] just sort of spiraled down the drain before we needed to put out another record. So that's when Rockie took the helm and started Cambodia Recordings.

RB: I basically decided that I wanted to put together a label that would just release Cleveland bands. I think I started it in '95 or '96. The first thing we put out was a Duvalby Brothers CD and then a 45 by a band called Biblical Proof of UFOs. I think the next thing was a Disengage 45, and then the fourth thing that we put out was *Map, Monitor, Surge*. Then we went on and we put out the Keelhaul record and the first Disengage CD and the first Red Giant record.

For me, I was in a position where I could fund a lot of this stuff from what I was doing professionally, and I just kind of wanted to do that for a while. It was cool; it was like a co-op, and anybody who was in these bands who wanted to would come and help collate packages to send out to radio and press packs and one-sheets, everybody pitching in and helping how they could. It was something I wanted to do, but there was too much of a business overhead that I didn't want to deal with to keep it legit — all the paperwork and taxes. It drove me nuts and burned me out pretty quick.

XIII. Map, Monitor, Surge

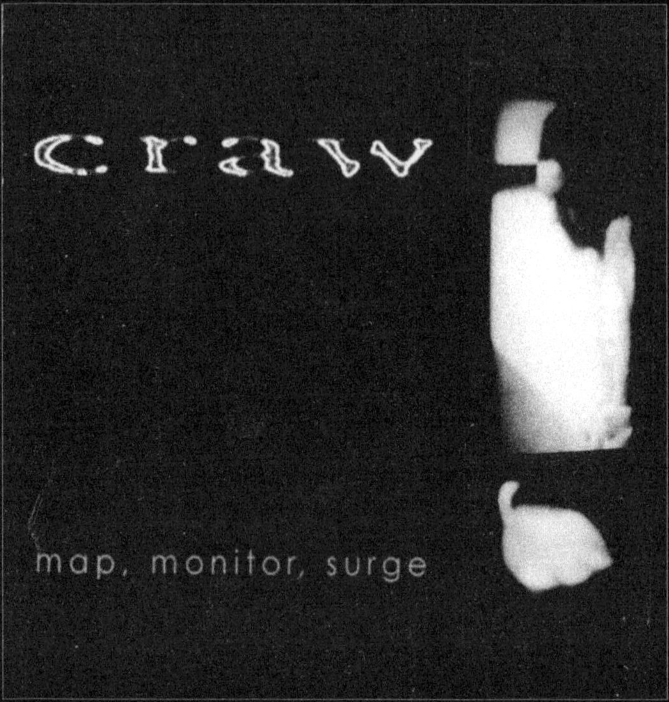

STEVE ALBINI (1997): I don't want to say the band [was] getting better, because they began on a pretty developed plateau of musicianship. But there's a greater degree of spontaneity in *Map, Monitor, Surge*. More was left to chance.

DM (1997): We're kind of at a point with this band where it's not, at least for me, so much about about pushing forward as it is about problem-solving. Like, we look at the last two albums and the written music, and we say, "That's kind of where we're coming from; this is the material we're coming up with now. How can we avoid making some of the mistakes that we did on the last album?"

It's just clarity of presentation, really, is what I and consciously I think most of us are trying to go for. So that if we have one musical movement going on, we don't have that movement going on but four other things distracting from it. And if a part is supposed to have a certain feeling that it does have that feeling and everyone's working toward it. What we're doing is clear to us, so it's kind of a problem-solving thing of how do we make it clear to other people.

We kind of kicked [Joe's] ass [on *Map, Monitor, Surge*]. We were basically like, "Sing on the beat, and sing with a little bit of melody." He could've gone further in that direction, but he went as far as he did, and I'm glad that he did.

At the same time we're doing this focusing thing, we're also trying to do the entropic thing of putting forward as much information as possible. There's tons of words; there's tons of ideas; there's tons of musical ideas; there's musical ideas that go in many different directions. But what we're trying to do is, with each of those things, each song, each musical concept, to focus that particular concept. So that's why you have the little tiny songs that repeat themselves, the couple really long songs.

ZD: My songs on *Map, Monitor, Surge* were "Unsolicited, Unsavory"—or "The Hit Single," as I like to refer to it—and "I Am Gunk," which totally did not turn out the way I had envisioned it. ["I Am Gunk"] was one where everybody put in their two cents and by the end, it wasn't exactly what I wanted it to be.

We called ["Unsolicited, Unsavory"] "Dubbie." Around the time I wrote that, I was into Bill Laswell, and I was listening to some of his dub stuff, so that's what influenced that [bass-and-drums breakdown].

JM: "Unsolicited, Unsavory" is as lapsed Irish Catholic as it gets, starting with a meditation on guilt and regret, moving on to some repressed sexuality and ending with a confessional.

"I Am Gunk" is my homage to J.G. Ballard.

"Divinity of Laughter" and "Days in the Gutter / Nights in the Gutter" both owe a debt to George Bataille. "Divinity of Laughter" is a chapter title in Bataille's *Guilty*, and I was empathetic with his quest to find the sacred even in the absence of God. With "Days in the Gutter / Nights in the Gutter," I wanted to combine a day in the (gutter) life with this aspiration to transcend our hero's situation. Also, the humor of a dedicating a song to gutter-cleaning was not lost on Dave or me.

RB: We wanted to record at Bill's new place. He had built this new studio; I think we had done "Cancerman" there, or something. It was a great studio. He had a super-high-tech Neve [console]—48-track, floating faders. All this really cool stuff. This gigantic room with, I forget what type of wood it was, but it just sounded fantastic. And so I asked Steve if he'd be interested in coming out to Cleveland to record at this place, and he was like, "Yeah, man, no problem." So he ended up staying at my place for six days. And Bill's studio was a good 45 minutes south of Cleveland, so we would make that trek every day. We did it in the winter, so there was bad snow driving for 45 minutes each way; spend like 10 to 14 hours in the studio and drive back. It was taxing, but it was a lot of fun.

This was the first time we'd recorded a full-length recording in a big, wide-open space where everybody was in the same room. We'd done a bunch of the singles, the one-offs, in a lot of these rooms. Craw's always been a very visual-cued band, so in the studio, I think that helped a lot.

ZD: As far as a recording situation, *Map, Monitor, Surge* is probably my proudest moment [in terms of craw] as a band. I can go back and listen to that record now and hear some of the mistakes we made on it. At the time, my aesthetic was that we should be able to play all these songs live pretty much in one take. We didn't do everything in one take, but I'd say 75 percent of that album was in one take. That was definitely our tightest moment as a band. Even [*Bodies for Strontium 90*], which was considerably easier to play than anything on *Map Monitor, Surge*, I don't think we recorded any of that album in one take. But *Map, Monitor, Surge*, we just banged 'em out.

Mars Studio is way nicer than Steve's basement. I think at the time, Steve was probably just getting together his big studio that he has now, but I don't think it was up and running. And Korecky had just gotten his new super-fancy console with the automated faders, so we all didn't have to stand around the board pushing each other's faders up and down. And we're good friends with Bill and liked working with him. Mars Studio has this huge oak or something room [where] we could all play in the same room and space amplifiers away from each other so there wasn't too much bleedthrough. It was just a lot better situation than what Albini had in his basement.

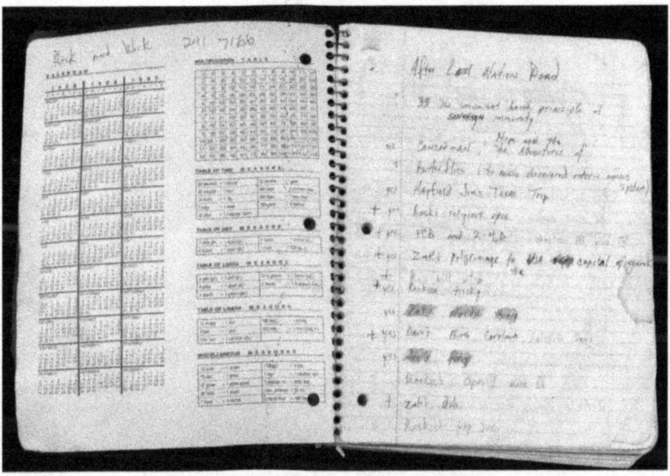

Interlude: "Shorties"

RB: I still love those three [short] songs. Those were Dave's. They were fantastic.

DM: I like the shorties. Maybe that's the most successful thing [I wrote for craw]. I was like, "Oh, Rockie's writing these enormous songs? I'm going to write a very short song." So I wrote a song that was a minute. And I was like, "Oh, I can just take this, and instead of going A-B-C-D-E-F, I can go A-B1-C1-D1, A-B2-C2-D2 and come up with three different songs and put them all together. And for me, it directly goes back to "Flying Houses," [from] Scratch Acid's *Berserker*. It's in three parts, with these huge pauses. So there was a punk-rock precedent for it. But at the same time, it's like, "This is a horn part." The line is like an alto sax part, so there's that specifically jazz thing happening.

I think for those songs, I literally was like, "I'm going to write a song that's a minute long, and it's going to be very complex." I can kind of remember doing it—coming up with all this material and going piece by piece, and thinking to myself, "Jesus, that's not even a minute. I guess I've got to do some repetition to actually hit a minute." We learned that one and we recorded it with Matt [Dufresne] for the *CLE Magazine* compilation, and then I came up with two other ones. And also, to me, that's just really funny: to write three songs that all start exactly the same that are a minute long.

JM: The sources for those songs were an intersection of biochemistry and genetic memes. My dad and I were rehashing some incomplete family history, and he remarked how he would have liked to go back in time and be a fly on the wall, enabling the ability to compare current family attitudes and mannerisms with those from the past. My interest in biochemistry started with the AIDS epidemic, and then to viruses in general.

When I read about night soil men, "green" plastic and modified genomes, the lyrics fell into place.

X

Dave's III

I My dear old dad is a new strain
of parasitic man

II The ace up his sleeve
is the unresearched exflagellation
factor

III He evades all attempts
by the man to interrupt
his progenys sporogony

their goal is to modify the ability of his
target population to transmit him along

IV Biochemists desire to insert exogeneous
DNA into his very genome

1. So they hired an infectous agent

2. to carry the anti-parasite gene

3. in a rapid transformation sweep

I' So whats his legacy, after all
is said and done?

II' Just name me a Zygote after all
I'm just my dads son

Treading Out the Winepress

We were just kids
Convincing ourselves we had seen
St Francis' statue move
They ran ahead of me
Ran out of the sacristy laughing

I knew a real archangel once
All nipping away at the pain of laughter
Listening from the core of quiet to the despair
That lies at the bottom of your heart
They are the winds
The thoughts between the hours that keep you at bay

And in that prophetic year
For forty days and seven hours
I witnessed
The multitudes freed
Against the Freemasons, the Mafia, and the KKK
I fought bathed in the glory of his light
I fought the false teachers who chose the way of Herod

A nigh-unto-naked boy holds a bowl of grapes
Smell the ozone when he speaks
Taste that fatted calf when he speaks,
"Every time a suctioner dies,
another one gets his wings."

Proud and brazen
All baleful and stinking
Whose throats should be slit-
Under cursed oath

The three women who were Herod's minions
Stood up in slow motion
They repeated what the demon said
To our lord at Capernaum
"What do you want of us? Have you come to destroy us?
We know who you are."

And so I felt his presence guide me
And thus my mind knew no quarrel with itself
And my right hand was steadied by him
And I flashed back to the firing range
And I testified unto them
Blest are they who show mercy
Mercy shall be theirs
But you have chosen to lead others astray
This is what you get
You should have prayed the rosary
I was called here
To tread out the winepress
And as I was cutting my hair afterward
I heard a voice say, "She'll feel it in her heart
And in her spine
With every remaining breath."
And another said, "Eloi, eloi, lama sabachthani."

Unsolicited, Unsavory

Invariably
The present eludes our hero
Chewing on
What's forgotten by most
As if it was an old split bone

Spinning endless circles
He repeats epics of his past glories
Such as this little gem
Again and again and again

Becoming progressively more unhinged
Undeviating
Unsound
Unlikely
But not unlike a rabid thing
Tied to a tree
I finally reckoned
With the very human need
For a little solace
I could call my own

Yet still from time to time
And this being one of them
My senses flower
Into a hyper-sensitivity
The heavy curtain is opened
The seven veils are dropped
The dull wallpaper of this sterile motel
Starts to shimmy
Not unlike that of your chemise
Standing near the delicate roses of your feelings
I inhale a specific scent
A stink of innocence
Wafting a warning
That for you my discourse
Is no longer tied to any gold standard

Holding the fragile orchid of your sentiment

Spinning circles
The whole room is indeed spinning
Spinning circles
The whole room is indeed spinning

Looking up at a ceiling
Merry-go-round slows to a stop
She bends over me
And simply asks,
"Have you ever
raped anyone?
Have you ever?"

I Disagree (And Here's Why)

The year twenty
And upwards of 30 days
Before I felt my secret
Come on the sly
Every inch of my body
Felt twisted
Stained by that sweetness

My skin crawls
As I watch my reflection
In the mirror

Saying to myself you
Stupid boy

As long as nobody touches me I'm fine
Riding each nightmare
Laughing

Scars have the power
To remind us that the past is real
Scars have the power to remind us that the past is real
Scars have the power to remind us that the past is real
Scars have the power to remind us that the past is real

Thus began my present fear of fire
Marking myself in his name
They can never forget
The early smell of burning flesh
Hanging below the heavy incense
Laying down to sleep each night
I try in vain
To thwart my secret
So conscious
Lost in reverie
That'll never help realize
What I hope for

The headaches and hot flashes
Keep me strong
Between the spells of unconsciousness

During the late shift
The nurse had said that there resides
Some remarkable qualities
In the will of mankind

May I say
That she doesn't see
Anything like I do

May I say
I'm the only one
Who put me in this condition
May I say
This string of events
Is beyond hilarity

May I say
There's nothing noble
Being reduced to burnt meat
And may I say
That she doesn't see anything
Like I do

Rip and Read

Signal demodulated
In propagating
Through the usual irregular channels

Degradations occurred
Due to nonlinearities

Spontaneous fluctuations detected

PR designed
To add shot and thermal noise
To the clean signal

Through the envelope detector
Wait I think I've got it all
Quantizing the noise
Utilizing the threshold effect

Here it is
The source is obviously a deep-cover contact

Canned by Carter
Relocated off-shore
Fed a false positive
To the media darling
Perfect parroting the proper diversions
Away from the cowboys

The media darling sets the satellite coordinates
And downlinks the following dogshit
Into the transducer:

"My fellow receivers
The time has come to modulate the appropriate response
What we desire
Is not a clearer reception
Nor greater resolution of the big picture
But to have the courage to admit
And the energy to act on it
That what we need
Is more man-made noise.
This marks the new era.
Bury the signal
Underneath the noise--
"This marks the new era."

I Am Gunk

The new law clearly states that the high-level waste
Must undergo vitrification
A process that mixes glass with the gunk
In order to stabilize the stuff
We came from the Savannah River Plant in South Carolina
We came from the Fernald Feed Materials Production Center in Ohio
We came from the Y-12 plant in Tennessee
We came from the Mound Facility in Texas

I first heard of the hoary mess at Hanford
Because of the federal raid on Rocky Flats
One billion dollars a year cleaned up
Compelling me to make that pilgrimage
Marveling at the majestic storage tanks
Numbering one hundred and seventy-seven
Each the size of the U.S. Capitol Dome
Containing what can only be referred to as gunk

I intentionally wandered
Like a particle during Brownian movement
Though I noticed the surround motion sensors
Not noticing me

Reacting and reforming
The gunk eludes any description
At any one time
The technicians can't ascertain
The sludge's composition
With any certainty

And therefore it ain't going to be vitrified
And therefore the new law is a joke
And it occurs to me the real reason
Why I am here
In a way I am to be vitrified

The stuff we're dealing with can't be wished away
It can only decay
You can containerize it
Solidify it
Immobilize it or move it
But it won't just go away

Clean controlled stable
Eleven kilograms
Creates a
Potentially unsafe geometry
Near enough to be labeled a criticality-infraction
Creating a natural sacrifice area
There's not nearly enough money in the world
Unclean
Uncontrolled
Unstable

Vitrification is our salvation
I will be vitrified
Vitrification is our salvation

Killer Microbes Devour Cleveland

My great-granddad was a night soil man, which he meant he fed shit to microorganisms. I feed them something a little different. I feed them PCBs. I feed them 2-4d. I teach them to eat everything.

Which may sound sinister, but trust me when I say, it's ok; it's all right; it's benign.

Without their artificial environment, they just die.

Step right up and see natural selection.

New Plastics Diet Alters Man's DNA

My ill-fated granddad was a plastic man, which meant he developed a microbe's taste for synthetic substances by shuffling his very DNA.

The industry liked him, because he was dirt-cheap and delivered a nice detoxified end-product.

The inevitable famine brought on new appetites. He would then exchange entire chunks of genetic material, to be the only one able to digest 2-4d by himself.

So, with me at his feet, this is what he always said: "Mutate and survive."

Parasitic Dad Evades Biocops

My dear old dad is a new strain of parasitic man. The ace up his sleeve is the unresearched exflagellation factor. He evades all attempts by the Man to interrupt his progeny's sporogony.

Biochemists desire to insert exogeneous DNA into his very genome. Their goal is to modify the ability of his target population to transmit him along. So they hired an infectious agent to carry the anti-parasitic gene in a rapid transformation sweep.

So what's his legacy, after all is said and done? Just name me a zygote.

After all, I'm just my dad's son.

Divinity of Laughter

Where in the hell am I?
Where in the hell's that map?

Thrown and abandoned
Stuck on seeing
Fate's fatiguing hand in everything
Don't really know
Where the self-imposed weight originates

Yet I ain't going to live
The rest of my life
Every live-long day
Every infinite hour
Fixated on my epitaph
Or calculating a premature end
I ain't going to live the rest of my life
Forever
Grinding
Misfortune's axe

Later in a weaker moment
I catch myself
Anguishing over phantoms

Something more is needed
A violent divine convulsion
A strange form of success
That re-arranges the world
So pile on the abuse
Off I'll go howling at the world

Never sacrificing levity
In the pursuit of clarity

Re-assembling the nonsense
One light-hearted moment at a time

Hayfield Jim's Texas Trip

Hayfield Jim fled to Texas, to take what now he could take. With his wife-to-be Lenore at the wheel, he got this, his best offer yet. For three thousand dollars, he ingested daily experimental pharmaceuticals of various colors and persuasions administered by apparent professionals. Hayfield Jim did not seem to feel that this was a bad thing.

But he could not leave. He had to be observed until forty times the sun circled the earth. And so his true love Lenore languished. And she took another to her breast. And when she called him at the clinic, she said to him, "Hayfield Jim, I hate to wait for anyone, or anything."

And soon after, Jim was released. And soon after, the fog lifted from his eyes. And soon after, he extinguished her new flame. So crazed for her was he that it took eight peace officers to bear him away. The bail was set at exactly three grand.

Creating the New Paranoid Man

Solid motor ejection
Thor Rocket Septaration
Agena ignition
Initiate photo ops
Hidden inside a milk factory
In Needham, Massachusetts
The powers that be gave us
An extension of three months

To build the impossible

The damn acetate cracked endlessly
A corona was cast on every photograph
The spin rockets kept blowing up
And in the end
All the components were built from scratch

Control freaks are now imitating
The worst in past Soviet practices
The public paid for the Corona Satellites
We now demand maximum access

Plenty of missions
Plenty of glitches
Errant film canisters
Ended up with Russian woodcutters

Pitch down
Heat shield Septaration
Deceleration chute
And air recovery

Days in the Gutter/ Nights in the Gutter

On autopilot
Fall out of bed
At exactly 7:13 am every day
The same dream
About slime on cement lingers
Fed the meter
Caffeine hits the bottom of the belly
Nicotine fills the sinuses
Hell I don't mind working alone

Good morning ma'am
I've come to clean your gutter
And flush your downspouts
Grey skies and barren trees
Are truly beautiful things

Check the number twice
Set up the humiliator against the roof
Hook the bucket onto the belt
Plant both feet deep into the trough
Pull out the cage
And pound out the muck
The slop of ammonia makes a fine cologne

Three years I've worked the gutter trade
A series of accidents and here I am
Insanely in love with chance

Now comes the time for all good men
To give endless praise
To the delights of friction

Yeah you might consider me a little thick
And might wonder which character flaw
Brought me to such a lowly station

(Chim-chimney chim-chim chiree)
I see things differently
Chim-chimney chim-chim chiree

I'm a one-man gutter-cleaning machine

I shouldn't be up on this fucker
Every step on the moss covered wood
Every awkward sweep into the bucket
Feels like I'm destined for the dirt

(Chim-chimney chim-chim chiree)
Where does it come from?

This urge to end the tension
To take the flailing leap
To really test the body's limits

Teetering
Teetering

Nearly losing my shit

(Chim-chimney chim-chim chiree)

A glance down
I spy a hook
A snow angel
And it looks like dumb luck

If by cruel chance I misstep
If by a stroke of luck
A snow angel does snare me

Then bring on twilight

Catatonic
Faces are masks
Hiding a leer or a sneer

Twilight's over

Nights in the gutter
Each one feels like Fat Tuesday gone wrong
And often times
Your hat, wallet and pride desert you

Directing delirium
Somehow
To stand what's dreary and irrelevant
On its head

Yeah give me a drink that'll put me on the floor

Now is the time for all good men
To sing alleluias to the joys of friction
Purposely seeking out
Exhaustion and disappointment
Just because I can
Just for the sake of variety
Oh the many flavors of excess
And their consequences
Peace and relaxation
Are impossible for you now

Sharing a mutual laceration
We'll enter the region of dreams
An unreal game
That must exist
Playing with attraction and anxiety
Gambling that beyond the nausea
Something akin to lightning would strike us

Sharing a mutual laceration
We'll dismantle the mechanical
Lover
You could always be respectable
Enjoying the esteem of the servile
Always cautious, a mere shadow
I have a child's hope
That you'll be able
To recall impulses
From your girlhood
That would now disrupt the trivial

We'll find more ways than just existing
Sending alleluias
To the inhuman stars!

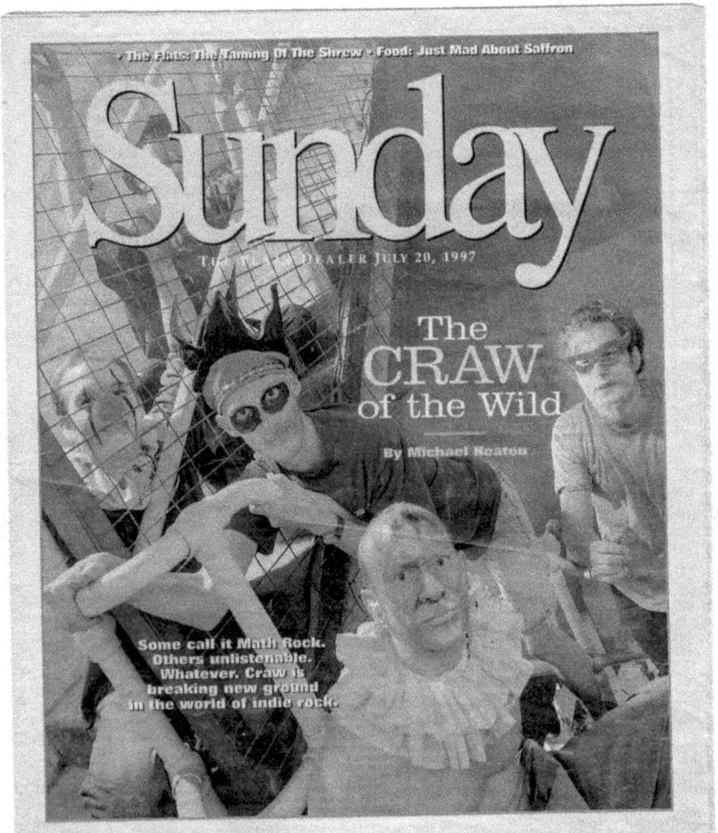
• The Flats: The Taming Of The Shrew • Food: Just Mad About Saffron
Sunday
DEALER JULY 20, 1997
The CRAW of the Wild
By Michael Heaton
Some call it Math Rock. Others unlistenable. Whatever. Craw is breaking new ground in the world of indie rock.

LETTERS

To The Editor

VIOLENT VIDEO GAMES

Re: "Apocalypse Now," by Edmund Guy (July 13).

Guy was unable to face the effects on our youth of the violent video games he described in his article. Like other apologists for violent media, he clung to the point that, after all, many kids who play these games grow up just fine. This reasoning ignores the common-sensical fact that no single factor completely determines life outcomes for young people, and the real question is whether a given factor makes it *more* or *less* likely that a life will turn out well.

Research clearly indicates that extended use of violent video games makes this less likely. These games make young people more aggressive and willing to use violence, even causing *physiological* changes associated with aggression.

Of course, there are many youth who use drugs, skip school, join gangs and engage in unprotected sex who, nonetheless, eventually turn out just fine. But that doesn't mean these behaviors aren't harmful. Adults need to protect youth from all the risk factors that, together, do have a major impact on our children's future. As a child psychologist, I recommend that parents discourage child use of violent video games.

Jeremy Shapiro, Ph.D.
Director
Center for Research, Evaluation and Training
Applewood Centers Inc.
Cleveland

CRAW'S MUSIC JUST 'NOISE'

Michael Heaton calls Craw, a Cleveland underground band, "unlistenable bliss" ("The Craw Of The Wild," July 20).

I would call the band the maker of unbearable, hellish noise.

Its high decibels mean danger for a listener's ears and mind.

Fricis A. Rungis
Cleveland Heights

Letters will be considered for publication only if accompanied by your full name, address and daytime telephone number. We edit for length and clarity. Concise letters are more likely to be published. All submissions become the property of The Plain Dealer and will not be returned; submissions may be published or otherwise used in any medium.

XIV. McClelland departs

RB: We were starting to write a little bit of new material. We did some little experimental things. There's something that Dave wrote which [had] a whole bunch of weird, noisy keyboard stuff going on.

DM: The song was called "I'm a Star." We'd had these talks about doing a pop album that were kind of serious, so in my mind, I was writing a pop song for craw. There had already been a lot of friction over the keyboard thing. To me, it was an extension of other electronics I was using at that time. If I'd had more money, I would've been able to come up with something that made more sense.

But that song, the recorded version had problems. There's a drum machine; there's Will sped-up; there's a bunch of different stuff. I feel like it was under-rehearsed because people weren't excited about it, which is fair. It sounded rough, but on the other hand, Will does great, interesting things on it; Joe does great, interesting things that are not what he usually does. And I really like the heavy [verse] riff. I thought that was a heavy melody; I thought that could be a pop thing for craw.

So we walked out of that studio and in the end, maybe I felt like I wasted money and time and tape by doing this, so I felt like, "If I've just pushed this whole thing in the wrong direction, I'm sorry about that."

We had just had this horrible tour. I think there was another tour after the Season to Risk tour. Rockie was like, "I'm not going to tour again. I have this job." And I was like, "Well, I don't want to live in Cleveland." So I was planning to move, and we were having these conversations about, "Well, there's this thing called the Internet, and you can send tapes back and forth, and that could possibly happen." But we weren't having conclusive conversations.

RB: Dave and I had a little run-in one night during rehearsal. He was out of tune, and I told him to go tune his guitar, and I was maybe more of a dick about it than I needed to be. And he said, "Fuck you people—I'm not going to be in this band anymore." So then it all came to a head. There were a few primary reasons. He was thinking about moving to New York anyway.

DM: At a certain point, we had this practice and Rockie got shitty with me and I was like, "I'm just fuckin' leaving." I was like, "I'm leaving anyway, but I'm just going to leave [the band]." To me, when I look back on it, it was that classic thing of, you're having a hard time with your significant other, you get in a fight, and oh, now we're going to break up because we had this horrible fight. So that's what it was to me. They obviously weren't going to be a touring band. I obviously wasn't going to live in Cleveland with this band that wasn't touring because I didn't want to live in Cleveland, and that was that.

I look back on it and I wish things had gone differently in one way and then on the other hand, I'm like, "Well, that's the way it was." It's not even that I wish I had been on [*Bodies for Strontium 90*]; it's more that I just wish that we hadn't been dumb about it. Looking back on it, we should've just said, "We're taking a break."

XV. Bodies for Strontium 90

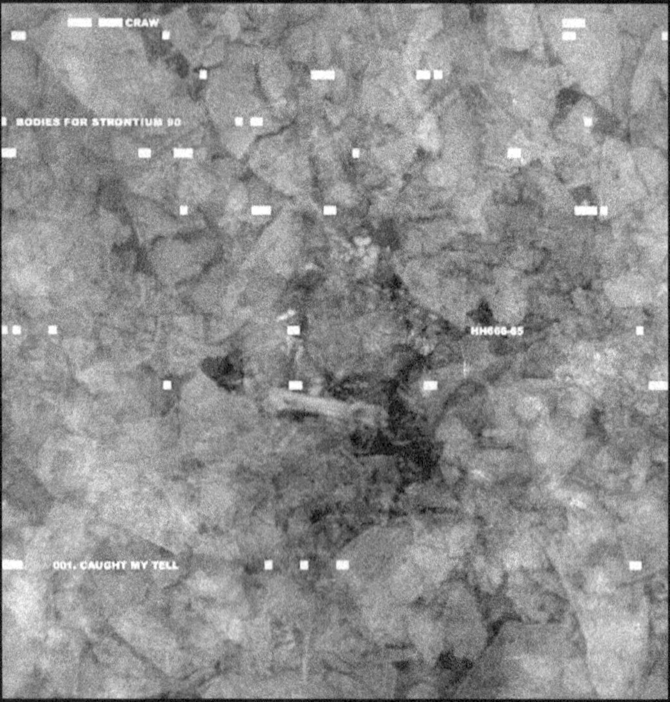

RB: I don't think we were really sure what we were going to do [after Dave left]. We weren't sure if we were going to do anything more. And then Keelhaul hooked up with Hydra Head, and it turns out that once they realized that Will also drummed in craw, they wigged out. They were big craw fans. They were just like, "You're going to write a new record, right? We'll put it out." And we were just like, "Okay—we can do that." So we did.

AARON TURNER (HYDRA HEAD RECORDS): I think the first time I actually heard [craw] was when I saw them play at the Middle East upstairs in Boston. It must have been '96, '97. With a lot of bands, I feel like the lack of familiarity with recorded output makes it harder to get into them when you see them live, but craw was one of those things where the first time I saw it, it just completely blew me away. I'd never heard anything quite like craw up to that point, and I'd definitely never seen anything like that live. They were this strange mixture of noise-rock and metal with this very eccentric, preacher-type character doing these weird pseudo-sermons over the top of the music. It was just a very potent concoction of elements. That was the beginning of my infatuation with craw. I bought a couple of their records at the merch table that night and a weird bright-yellow T-shirt with silver ink on it, which was fitting given how weird their music was. I was a devout follower from then on.

Once I saw them, I became pretty fascinated with their music. I bought everything they had at the table that night, and then I spent quite a bit of time trying to track down the other records. *Lost Nation Road* was one that really got me—there was something about that record. The atmosphere of that particular record really drew me in. It's like this constantly surging, undulating thing that sucks you in, and all the little guitar lines and intricate drum fills feel like these weird tendrils that interlock with each other and overlap and wrap around inside your skull. One of the things that I look for in a record is when there's a strong sense of atmosphere, and that record has so much atmosphere to it. It wasn't a really opaque darkness, but it was definitely sinister without being overly dramatic. And there was also this weird almost absurdist edge to it too, without it being comical. I think that has a lot of do with Joe's voice and his vocal delivery. The music was a little more stern and stone-faced, and Joe was this really bizarre element thrown into the mix that somehow oddly worked. It was a good juxtaposition. It was a very compelling but also unsettling listening experience.

[Craw's music] was related to [metal and hardcore], but it couldn't be clearly assigned any of those genres or subgenres, and I think that was one of the things that really appealed to me. I remember from one of the first times I saw them live how interesting all the interplay between the instruments were. It's fairly typical in a lot of metal or hardcore for both guitars to be playing unison or at least doing harmonies off of each other. There were points where [Rockie and Dave] locked in on certain things, but very often, they were doing these completely different things that somehow worked very well. Things were interwoven rather than just stapled together.

Will's drumming too was definitely a jaw-dropping thing to behold. In a certain way, it was reminiscent of other metal drumming in that it was flamboyant and very fast, but it was very chaotic. The interesting thing about it was that even though it looked like things were on the verge of falling apart, it also felt very cohesive. It was like a shuddering locomotive going down the tracks and pieces of it are flying off in all directions, but it stays on a very steady, straight course.

Because of the heaviness of craw, I was instantly able to relate to what they did, but also, it gave me something new or something that was very unique. It was a thing unto itself, and I appreciated that. And I appreciated the visual aesthetic of the band in the live setting. There wasn't any pretense; they just did it. They put a lot of passion into the performance, but there was no grandstanding at all. They kept their head down and did their thing.

The visual aesthetic of the albums were interesting too. Again, it had a darkness that I could relate to from my metal and hardcore background, but it also didn't clearly state itself as one thing or another.

The lyrics had a very abstract quality to them. While you could tell what [Joe] was talking about, it wasn't clearly spelled out. There wasn't a clearly defining theme that ran throughout them all; it was these very well-constructed but chaotic ramblings. And that set it apart from a lot of the normal metal stuff as well.

If I remember correctly, it was actually because of Keelhaul that [Hydra Head] decided to work with craw. I had been a fan of craw for a long time, but somehow, it had never occurred to me to ask them about doing a record. The relationship with Keelhaul developed and working with craw seemed like the next logical step, since craw was what had brought me to Keelhaul to begin with.

I did the artwork for *Bodies*, but other than that, it was really just striking a deal and agreeing to work together and telling them to just kind of have at it. [Touring] certainly wasn't something we were concerned about; we were just excited to do a record with them.

WS: It was pretty simple: Dave said, "I'm moving to New York," and we continued on as a four-piece. It became more of a rock band. We had to adapt. We still wanted to play. For better or for worse, we're gonna keep doing this, and we're gonna make another record, so let's go down in the basement and practice.

At that point, I think our set consisted mostly of newer stuff, from the last record, and we didn't play that much old stuff. We did play some old stuff, and Rockie had to tailor the guitar parts. We had to figure out what songs we could do. I think the person it was hardest on was Rockie, because there were points where Dave's guitar parts were more key to the song than [his], so he was like, "Fuck, which part am I gonna play, mine or Dave's?" But he figured it out.

It definitely changed the sound of the band, because Dave almost functioned more like a keyboard player would. He was playing stuff that's like—I hate using words like "atmospheric," but he was the texture guy, the layer guy, like putting this crazy, wacky, weird, interesting, cuckoo thing over what would ordinarily be a bunch of chugging and riffing. And I like a bunch of chugging and riffing; I'm a metalhead, so that's fine with me. But when you add the extra layer on, it's like, "Wow, a cake with frosting—who would've thought of that?" It's sprinkles on a cupcake, and Dave was the sprinkles.

AARON TURNER: For whatever [*Bodies*] lost in density or complexity, it became catchier. The songs had a more memorable quality to them. Whereas the other records seemed like these long, epic pieces that were broken up into smaller chunks, *Bodies* sounded more like a set of clearly defined songs; it had more of the pummeling energy that I'd experienced in the live setting. As far as records that Hydra Head put out over our 15-plus-year existence, that's one that I can go back to and still really, really enjoy. It still sounds really relevant to me.

ZD: As records go, [*Bodies*] was probably the most discussed record. All the other music was sort of, everybody gets to do their own thing with their own songs, and everybody else has to agree to that principle, that craw's an open band where everybody gets to explore their own musical path. But with *Bodies*, for one thing, Will, Rockie and I had definitely always been more on the same hard-rock/metal track than Dave was, and we talked about how we wanted to make a rock album of just songs that we would play live. Because so many of the songs on the other records that had big dynamic shifts and were long and had lots of changes ended up not being that fun to play live. So we discussed that we wanted to make an album of songs that we will want to play every night. Even though we weren't touring and were never going to play them, ever! So it was going to be our rock record.

I know from my standpoint, I wrote a lot more songs on *Bodies* than on the other records. And I always tried to be cognizant of Dave not being in the band in the songs I wrote; I tried to write parts that would be cool for Rockie. Because I wrote everything at this point on guitar. So I tried to write parts for Rockie to play that also had some high-end on it too, so we didn't turn into this super sludge band with two bass players, one of them just playing guitar.

RB: Everything [on *Bodies*] was done at Bill's studio. We were going for something thicker, heavier, more metal. And that was really Bill's thing. The early craw records, even though sonically they sounded amazing with Steve at the helm, weren't as heavy as I liked. And there was absolutely the argument that if they were any heavier, then they probably wouldn't sound as good. But having then the opportunity to write a craw record that was really kind of crushing, I took every advantage of that.

XVI. Ending

ZD: I don't really remember [how the band ended]. Not that we didn't want to tour anymore, but life had occurred, so we weren't going to be able to tour anymore without using up our two weeks of vacation time a year. Probably somebody said, "I can't really do this anymore. I've got to get a real job." I think around that time, Joe had taken a real job as an electrical engineer, and Rockie was being more serious with his work. And obviously, Will wants to tour for the rest of his life, but it wasn't going to be in craw. I think I was still working in crappy bike-shop or painting-houses jobs and could've done anything, but I was married and my wife was sort of like, "Yeah, this is enough of this."

RB: For me, I think [ending the band] seemed like more of a natural life progression. I was several years into my own company, and that was taking a large amount of time. And if I had made a career to decision to start my own company and not tour, then of course Joe can make a decision to follow his career and move [away from Cleveland].

XVII. Summation

WS: I got a shitload out of playing with craw, because I learned so much about what was possible with music that I don't know if it would occur to most people. Just that you can fuck with [music], and things don't have to be in groups of four and eight and 16, and you can take something that's in this time signature and butt it right up against something that's this, and then leave a weird space here, and turn this upside down and play this on [its] head. You can just do wacky stuff—the possibilities are endless. You don't have to be confined by everybody else's idea of a rock song, or any kind of a song, or just music.

NC: That all-for-one and one-for-all mentality and belief in the music and vision of the music led us to be able to do a lot of pretty cool things. A lot of traveling, a lot of presenting this music to people through shows and through our recordings, and that's a wonderful thing to be a part of.

DM: At a certain point, around the second album, I realized that the three things that we were trying to do, or the three things I liked about the band, were that we were visceral, intellectual and emotional. I would say to Joe that we're trying to operate on the visceral, which is why we would be so loud and so heavy, have all the low frequencies. And we were trying to operate on the [intellectual], which is why we'd be giving you stuff to think about in the music and in the lyrics. And then we would try to operate on the emotional, which would come through especially in Joe's delivery and our commitment to delivering onstage. We would try to stack all those three things up.

JM: I was too close to music to determine objectively if it was a success. The amount of dopamine after a show or recording distorted judgement.

Simply performing the songs live enough times enabled confidence. The pressure of performing live molded the song into something more than just five sonic layers. Shows were exhilarating when the band was on fire and so was the audience.

EXIT
COUNTRY!

ZD: Not everything worked, but if you're an experimental band, not everything's going to work. But every record has several songs on it that I think really got across what we were as a band at that moment in time. I definitely feel like we hit the nail on the head several times hard and I'm pretty happy about that.

RB: It's in my opinion a really strong, very creative body of work. And regardless of the times that may not have been as happy-go-lucky, there's absolutely a lot of pride that I feel when I look back at all that stuff.

CA: Craw, that was the experiment. The songwriting, the music experimentation and throwing something together that had a lot of power, energy and feel, that says everything. That was a lot of fun.

I love music; I love playing. It's funny, looking back, I haven't played in 20 years, since I was done with craw. I guess maybe it was just a transition in life and whatnot. But the best thing about music is playing out, playing music in front of people. When you go places and what you're playing is so mature—it's not polished; it's maturity—and when you can build the energy and the feel, and the crowd just soaks it up, the feeling you get is just amazing. If you can create that, in some ways, you're inviting people into your experience and they're enjoying that. And then you can feed off of that, and there's just this synergy.

When you're playing covers and certain canned styles, it's like, "Yeah, you know...," but when you write the music to try to create an experience people can feel, then they feel it, and then you're feeling that, and when that whole thing matures, I don't think there's anything better than that. Maybe that sums up craw.

And on top of that, I just love heavy music. And if I wasn't getting it the way I wanted it and I had to create it, then why not?

A timeline/discography

Notes: Items with asterisks are best-guess or otherwise uncertain.
If no city specified, show took place in Cleveland.

1988

FALL/WINTER, 1988–89

Chris Apanius, Rockie Brockway and David McClelland meet at Case Western Reserve orientation; begin rehearsals in Tippit House; perform as three-piece at dorm party. Joe McTighe joins; band settles on the name craw (originally formatted as C.R.A.W.), recruits drummer Lori Davis.

1989

WINTER/SPRING*

Shows at the Euclid Tavern, at JB's Down in Kent, OH, and outdoors at CWR.

1990

FEB 1*

Show at Thwing Center, Case Western Reserve.

FEB 14

Recording, probably at Tippit House practice space: "The Great American Bouzo [v. 1]," "X-President's Chordata," "PT Barnums Rubehead [v. 1]," "Onion Fucked-Out-Virus Ragman Targeted in Dizzyland Daisy Forget-Me-Not-March"

- All songs self-released on *craw* demo cassette, 1990

Chris Apanius - Bass, Rockie Brockway - Guitar, Lori Davis - Drums, David McClelland - Guitar, Joe McTighe - Vocals

FALL

Lori leaves Cleveland Institute of Art and craw. Neil Chastain joins; band moves practices to Staley House.

1991

FEB 18

Helmet show at the Euclid Tavern; craw members in attendance

UNKNOWN DATE

Recording at Modern Recordings with John Walsh:
"Raw Interface," "Bouzo [v. 2]," "Eidolons [v. 1]," "Wordfall [v. 1]," "Rubehead [v. 2]," "Gimme 12," "24 Hr. Live Bait Machine"

- All songs self-released on *Celephais* cassette, 1991

CA - Bass, RB - Guitar, Neil Chastain - Drums, DM - Guitar, JM - Vocals

Jun 3 - The Euclid Tavern with Haunting Souls and Love Battery
Jul 15 - The Euclid Tavern with Hammerhead
Sept 16 - The Euclid Tavern with Melvins

1992

Jan 27 - The Euclid Tavern with Tar, Unsane
Apr 1 - The Euclid Tavern

APRIL
Recording at Mars with Bill Korecky:
"Elliot [v. 1]," "My Sister's Living Room [v. 1]"
- Released on 7-inch (Hit & Run Records)

"Eidolons [v. 2]"
- Released on *Hotel Cleveland, Vol. 3* compilation (Scat)

"Tunnel Vision"
- Released on *3,128 Seconds Over Cleveland* compilation (WUJC, 88.7 FM); May, 1994.

"Marooned," "Shocklight [v. 1]," "Stomp [v. 1]"
Note: "Shocklight [v. 1]" is an early, radically different version of the song of the same name that appears on Lost Nation Road.
-All songs above self-released on *craw* demo cassette, 1992

CA - Bass, RB - Guitar, NC - Drums, DM - Guitar, JM - Vocals

Sept 1 - Peabody's DownUnder with Jesus Lizard, Tar, Jawbox

1993

JAN
Recording at Mars with Korecky:

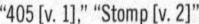

"405 [v. 1]," "Stomp [v. 2]"
- Released on 7-inch (Choke, Inc.; CHK-001)

CA - Bass, RB - Guitar, NC - Drums, DM - Guitar, JM - Vocals

Jan 10 - The Euclid Tavern with Season to Risk, Cher U.K.
Jan 25 - The Euclid Tavern with Janitor Joe, Ton
Mar 31 - The Euclid Tavern with Cop Shoot Cop

JUNE
Recording in Chicago with Steve Albini:
"Aphasia," "405 [v. 2]," "Cobray to the North," "1st Wednesday of the Month," "Elliot [v. 2]," "Moira Is Vanishing," "To the Child Reader," "Wordfall [v. 2]," "My Sister's Living Room [v. 2]," "Thinnest Line," "Stomp [v. 3]," "Echolocating," "Eidolons [v. 3]," "Slower"
-All songs released on *craw* CD/cassette (Choke, Inc.; CHK-002);

1993
(CONT.)

October, 1993. Contents reissued in *1993–1997* box.

CA - Bass, RB - Guitar, NC - Drums, DM - Guitar, JM - Vocals

Jul 25 - The Euclid Tavern with Alice Donut, Bluto's Revenge
Jul 28 - The Euclid Tavern with Dazzling Killmen, World Without End
Jul 31 - WRUW's Studio A-Rama festival, Case Western Reserve

SUMMER
Tour of the South, Midwest and West Coast
Note: included Seattle show with Voodoo Gearshift and Boneflower, as well as shows in Phoenix and Fort Worth.

Aug 10 - Minneapolis, MN; First Avenue with Myxx, Guru Stew, Wes ("New Band Showcase")
Oct 31 - The Euclid Tavern with Screwtractor, Eric's Mother, Drill Kitty, Boulder ("Pumpkinhead Halloween Party")
Nov 15 - The Euclid Tavern with Giant Metal Insects (Choke, Inc. release party for *craw*)

1994

WINTER/SPRING TOUR
Jan 10 - Cleveland
Jan 11 - Ann Arbor, MI, with Jaks, Zug Island Quartet
Jan 12 - Dayton, OH
Jan 14 - Pittsburgh, PA*
Jan 15 - Philadelphia, PA, with Kitchkao
Jan 16 - Asbury Park, NJ
Jan 21 - Huntington, WV
Jan 22 or 24 - Akron, OH, with Karma to Burn, Hyper as Hell*
Jan 23 - The Grog Shop with Milkmine, Duvalby Brothers
Jan 29 - Richmond, VA, with Hegoat
Feb 11 - Kent, OH
Feb 12 - Louisville, KY
Feb 16 - Columbus, OH
Feb 18 - Cleveland
Feb 19 - Morgantown, WV
Mar 3 - Chicago, IL
Mar 5 - Lexington, KY
Mar 11 - The Grog Shop with Johnboy, Supreme Dicks
Mar 12 - Kent, OH
Mar 17 - Lexington, KY
Mar 18 - Knoxville, TN

1994
(CONT.)

Mar 20 - Norfolk, VA
Mar 21 - New York, NY
Mar 22 - Buffalo, NY
Mar 23 - Philadelphia, PA
Mar 24 - Baltimore, MD
Mar 25 - Richmond, VA
Apr 1 - New Hampton, NY
Apr 2 - New York, NY
Apr 4 - The Euclid Tavern with Die Monster Die, Loppybogymi

SPRING
Derek Hess steps down as Euclid Tavern booker. Chris Apanius leaves band; Zak Dieringer joins.

Apr 15 - Dayton, OH
Apr 16 - Huntington, WV, at Gumby's with Torque, the Econothugs
April; unknown date - Pittsburgh, PA, with Karma to Burn
May 1 - Peabody's DownUnder with Prong, Course of Empire
Note: Some or all of the above shows were likely played without a bass player, while the band began rehearsing with Dieringer.
May 28 - Kent, OH

JUNE 10–13, 24–26
Recording, mixing in Chicago with Albini:
"Sound of Every Promise," "Strongest Human Bond," "Bypass," "Botulism, Cholera and Tarik," "Lifelike," "I Fought Dirty," "All This Has Made Me," "Shocklight [v. 2]," "Feesh Crik," "As Long as the Turnpike"
-All songs released on *Lost Nation Road* CD and, except for "I Fought Dirty," LP (Choke, Inc.; CHK-008); November, 1994. Contents reissued in *1993–1997* box.

-Marcus DeGrazia (then Marcus Rosinski) and Matt Dufresne play alto and baritone saxophone, respectively, on "Botulism, Cholera and Tarik" and "All This Has Made Me."

RB - Guitar, NC - Drums, Zak Dieringer - Bass, DM - Guitar, JM - Vocals

Jun 19 - Chicago, IL
Jul 2 - Kent, OH; Ozzie's
Jul 7 - Cleveland
Jul 8 - Dayton, OH

1994
(CONT.)

Jul 9 - Huntington, WV
Jul 17 - Baltimore, MD
Jul 18 - Asbury Park, NJ
Jul 20 - Boston, MA
Jul 21 - Portchester, NY
Jul 22 - New York, NY*
Jul 26 - Morgantown, WV, with Clutch
Jul 29 - Cincinnati, OH, with Milkmine
Jul 30 - Peabody's DownUnder with the Jesus Lizard, the Duvalby Brothers
July 31 - Richmond, VA, with Clutch
Aug 4 - Columbus, OH, with Hammerhead
Aug 5 - Toledo, OH
Aug 6 - Chicago, IL
Aug 20 - Detroit, MI, with Milkmine, Morsel, Jaks, possibly Hairy Patt Band (1994 Choke, Inc. Fest)
Oct 4 - Cleveland with Neurosis, Dazzling Killmen

UNKNOWN DATES, PROBABLY OCTOBER

Canada tour

UNKNOWN DATE, PROBABLY OCTOBER

One-off show in St. Louis, MO (Mississippi River Music Festival)

Dec 3 - Huntington, WV; Gumby's

1995

JAN 6

The Euclid Tavern with Tar (following Derek Hess / Karen Novak art show)

WINTER TOUR

Jan 28 - Columbus, OH; The Neil House (1473 Neil Ave) with Jaks
Jan 30 - Asbury Park, NJ; The Saint
Feb 1 - New York, NY; Brownie's with Deadguy
Feb 3 - New Brunswick, NJ, with Tow, Deadguy
Feb 4 - Baltimore, MD; Club Midnight with Thickshake
Feb 5 - Norfolk, VA*
Feb 7 - Richmond, VA; Citizen Gallery with King Sour
Feb 8 - Greensboro, NC; The Turtle with Bedwetter
Feb 9 - Cincinnati, OH; Sudsy Malone's Rock 'n Roll Laundry & Bar with Beel Jak, Ted Bundy's VW
Feb 10 - Lexington, KY; Wrockledge
Feb 11 - Nashville, TN; Lucy's

1995
(CONT.)

Feb 21 - Huntington, WV; The Drop Shop
Mar 3 - Athens, OH; Union
Mar 23 - St. Louis, MO; Cicero's
Apr 21 - Kansas City, MO; The Foundry with Season to Risk, Black Calvin (following "Censorship of Fools" art show at Recycled Sounds featuring Derek Hess)
Apr 22 - St. Louis, MO; Bernard's
Apr 23 - Memphis, TN; Barristers with Another Society
Apr 25 - Lake Charles, LA; Pourquoi Pas
Apr 26 - Lafayette, LA; Metropolis
Apr 27 - Panama City, FL; Mescalitos with Knucklefish
Apr 28 - Dothan, AL; Ramada Inn with Knucklefish, Gimcrack
Apr 29 - Pensacola, FL; Handlebar
May 1 - Athens, GA; Atomic
May 2 - Atlanta, GA; Somber Reptile
May 3 - Knoxville, TN; Mercury Theatre
May 4 - Chillicothe, OH; Blue Monk
May 5 - The Euclid Tavern with Dimbulb, Philo Beddow ("Home Opener"/"Fuck Baseball")
Jun 3 - Kalamazoo, MI
Jun 15 - Toronto, Ontario (NXNE Festival)
Jun 24 - New York, NY; Coney Island High with Unsane*
Jun 26 - Upstairs at Nick's; Philadelphia, PA
Jun 27 - Baltimore, MD; Club Midnight
Jun 28 - Washington, DC
Jun 29 - Richmond, VA; Twisters
Jun 30 - Norfolk, VA

Jul 12 - Columbus, OH; Stache's with Iceburn
Note: likely Neil Chastain's last show with craw

UNKNOWN DATE, AUG OR SEPT

Choke, Inc. folds.

Sept 3 - The Euclid Tavern with the Jesus Lizard ("Rock and Roll Hall of Fame Opening")
Note: first show with Will Scharf

GLAZED BABY TOUR

(a.k.a. "You Guys Play Like a Bunch of Girls Tour")
Sept 15 - Ypsilanti, MI; Green Room
Sept 16 - Chicago, IL; Fireside Bowl

1995
(CONT.)

Sept 18 - Madison, WI; O'Cayz Corral
Sept 19 - Minneapolis, MN; 400 Club
Sept 20 - Omaha, NE; Cog Factory
Sept 21 - Kansas City, MO; Graffiti Café
Sept 22 - Columbia, MO; garage show
Sept 23 - Nashville, TN; Lucy's
Sept 24 - Memphis, TN; Barristers
Sept 25 - Knoxville, TN; Mercury Theatre
Sept 26 - Chapel Hill, NC; Local 506
Sept 28 - Norfolk, VA; Kings Head Inn
Sept 29 - Baltimore, MD; Club Midnight
Oct 1 - Philadelphia, PA; Attic
Oct 2 - Asbury Park, NJ; The Saint
Oct 3 - New York, NY; Coney Island High
Oct 4 - Providence, RI; Met Café
Oct 6 - Boston, MA; The Middle East with La Gritona
Oct 7 - Old Town, ME; Heavies with with La Gritona
Oct 8 - Worcester, MA; Espresso Bar
Oct 9 - Portland, MN; Zoot's with La Gritona
Oct 11 - Montreal, Quebec
Oct 12 - Montreal, Quebec
Oct 13 - Ottawa, Ontario; 5 Arlington
Oct 14 - Toronto, Ontario; Rivoli
Oct 15 - London, Ontario; Embassy
Oct 16 - Buffalo, NY; Asbury Alley
Oct 17 - Pittsburgh, PA; Lucianas
Oct 18 - Youngstown, OH; Pyatt St. Pub
Oct 19 - Morgantown, WV; Nyabinghi with Neurosis
Oct 20 - Athens, OH; Union
Oct 21 - Kent, OH; Ozzie's

Dec 15 - The Euclid Tavern with Primitive

DEC; UNKNOWN DATE

Recording at Mars with Korecky:
"Cancerman" (a.k.a. "Hope and the Cancerman")
-released on *The Adventures of Cancer Man* 7-inch, including Derek Hess comic book (Super Model Records)

RB - Guitar, ZD - Bass, DM - Guitar, JM - Vocals, Will Scharf - Drums

1996

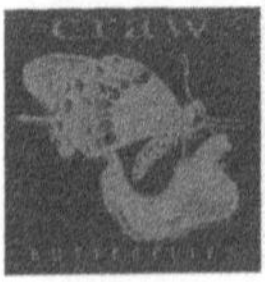

FEB; UNKNOWN DATE
Recording at Mars with Korecky:
"Butterflies"
- Released on craw/Primitive split 7-inch (No Lie Music; NL-013)

RB - Guitar, ZD - Bass, DM - Guitar, keyboard, JM - Vocals, WS - Drums, spoken-word vocals

Feb 17* - Peabody's DownUnder with Corrosion of Conformity, Gone in 60 Seconds
Feb 24 - Philadelphia, PA; Upstairs at Nick's
Feb 25 - New York, NY; Under Acme

MARCH; UNKNOWN DATES
Austin, TX; South by Southwest with Primitive (No Lie Music showcase)
Dallas, TX with Unsane

MARCH; UNKNOWN DATE
Recording at Mars with Korecky:
"Hayfield Jim's Texas Trip [v. 1]"
- Released on *Cleveland... So Much to Answer For* compilation (issued with *CLE Magazine No. 4*) and *The Good, the Bad and the Ugly* triple-7-inch compilation (Insolito; INSOLITO-06)

RB - Guitar, ZD - Bass, DM - Guitar, JM - Vocals, WS - Drums

Mar 16 - Kansas City, MO; The Daily Grind with Cheer-Accident, Quitters Club
Mar 29 - The Euclid Tavern with Throckmorton (Derek Hess "216" opening)
Jun 7 - Boston, MA; The Middle East with Cows, Poster Children, Ultra Bide, Quintaine Americana, Doc Hopper, Honkeyball, Bloodletter, Acid King, Michael Mancini ("Immaculate Destruction: The Rok Art of Derek Hess")
Jun 8 - Long Branch, NJ; Brighton Bar

AUG; UNKNOWN DATE
Recording at Mars with Korecky:
"New Plastics Diet Alters Man's DNA [v. 1]" (title listed as "Killer Microbes Devour Cleveland")
- Released on *Cleveland Squawks!* compilation (issued with *CLE Magazine No. 5*; CLECD3)

1996

(CONT.)

-Matt Dufresne plays baritone saxophone.

RB - Guitar, ZD - Bass, DM - Guitar, JM - Vocals, WS - Drums

Oct 31 - The Grog Shop with Duvalby Bros
Nov 27 - Cleveland with Disengage, Biblical Proof of UFOs

DEC; UNKNOWN DATE
Recording at Mars with Albini and Korecky:
"Treading Out the Winepress," "Unsolicited, Unsavory," "I Disagree (And Here's Why)," "Rip and Read," "I Am Gunk," "Killer Microbes Devour Cleveland," "New Plastics Diet Alters Man's DNA [v. 2]," "Parasitic Dad Evades Biocops," "Divinity of Laughter," "Hayfield Jim's Texas Trip [v. 2]," "Creating the New Paranoid Man," "Days in the Gutter / Nights in the Gutter"
-All songs released on *Map, Monitor, Surge* (Cambodia Recordings; CAM-004); May 10, 1997. Contents reissued in *1993–1997* box.

1997

RB - Guitar, ZD - Bass, DM - Guitar, JM - Vocals, WS - Drums

Apr 26 - Chicago, IL; Beat Kitchen with Disengage (Derek Hess "Strength Without Day-Glo" opening)

SEASON TO RISK TOUR
May 7 - Madison, WI; O'Cayz Corral
May 8 - Milwaukee, WI; Unicorn
May 9 - Chicago, Il; Fireside Bowl
May 10 - Euclid Tavern (*Map, Monitor, Surge* record release)
May 12 - Philadelphia, PA; Nick's
May 14 - Long Branch, NJ; Brighton Bar
May 15 - Boston, MA; The Middle East
May 17 - New Bedford, MA
May 19 - New York, NY; Under Acme
May 20 - Richmond, VA; Twisters
May 21 - Pittsburgh, PA; Beehive
May 22 - Huntingon, WV; Nyabinghi
May 24 - St. Louis, MO; Galaxy
May 25 - Kansas City, MO; Grand Emporium
May 27 - Kansas City, MO; Fusebox
May 28 - Kansas City, MO; Hurricane

1997
(CONT.)

May 30 - Denton, TX; Argo
May 31 - Austin, TX; Emo's
Jun 1 - Houston, TX; Emo's
Jun 3 - Ft. Worth, TX; Aardvark
Jun 4 - Witchita, KS; Kirby's Too (McClelland/Scharf duo covers set)
Jun 5 - Lawrence, KS; Replay Lounge
Jun 7 - Omaha, NE; with Ravine
Jul 16 - The Euclid Tavern with Iceburn, Verbena
Jul 22 - The Agora (Vans Warped Tour, local stage)

Sept 7 - Detroit, MI; Zoot's Coffee with Thoughts of Ionesco

Oct 3 - The Euclid Tavern with Disengage, Biblical Proof of UFOs (Brockway/McTighe/Scharf, billed as "Three Fifths Craw"; Derek Hess "Art Attack" opening)

DEC; UNKNOWN DATE

Recording at Mars with Korecky

"Chop Shop [v.1]"

- Released on *Decline of Midwestern Civilization* compilation (Ant Records / Violenteer Productions; ANT055) and *11: An Escape Artist Records Compilation* (Escape Artist Records; EA11.0)

"Space Is the Place [v. 1]"

- Released on craw/Sicbay split 7-inch (Obtuse Mule #405)

"I'm a Star"

- Unreleased

RB - Guitar, ZD - Bass, guitar on "Space Is the Place," DM - Guitar, bass on "Space Is the Place," keyboard on "I'm a Star," JM - Vocals, drum-machine programming on "I'm a Star," WS - Drums

1998

SPRING; UNKNOWN DATE

David McClelland leaves Cleveland and craw.

1999

Apr 17 - The Euclid Tavern with Ed Kemper Trio, Red Giant

May 15 - The Euclid Tavern

Oct 2 - Youngstown, OH; Nyabinghi with Meatjack

2000

Mar 17 - Youngstown, OH; Nyabinghi with Keelhaul
Mar 23 - The Blind Lemon with Isis, Anodyne, No Retreat

Oct 5 - The Euclid Tavern with Botch

Dec 16 - The Euclid Tavern with Nucleon, Rebreather, Positraction
(Children Who Witness Violence benefit)

2001

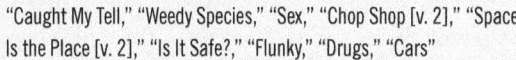

FEBRUARY
Recording at Mars with Korecky:
"Caught My Tell," "Weedy Species," "Sex," "Chop Shop [v. 2]," "Space Is the Place [v. 2]," "Is It Safe?," "Flunky," "Drugs," "Cars"
- All songs released on *Bodies for Strontium 90* CD (Hydra Head Records; H666-65) and LP (Radar Swarm; RSR-003)
-"Weedy Species" also released on *Music With Attitude, Volume 42* compilation (Rock Sound)
-Mike Callahan plays guitar on "Chop Shop."

"My Lacerations" (Dazzling Killmen cover)
-Released on *Digging Out the Switch Again: A Tribute to the Dazzling Killmen* (The Subversive Workshop)

RB - Guitar, ZD - Bass, JM - Vocals, WS - Drums

Sept 14 - Pittsburgh, PA; 31st St. Pub with Keelhaul, Nob

Oct 13 - The Euclid Tavern (Karen Novak photo opening)

2002

Mar 9 - The Grog Shop with Mastodon, Alabama Thunder Pussy,
Lick Golden Sky

Mar 24 - The Agora with Coalesce, The Esoteric, Premonitions of War

Apr 2 - The Beachland with Sicbay
Apr 5 - Youngstown, OH; Nyabinghi with Sicbay

DEC; UNKNOWN DATE
Joe McTighe leaves Cleveland; craw goes on indefinite hiatus.

2010

Aug 30 - The Euclid Tavern with Unsane, Non Fiction
(Brockway/Dieringer/Scharf; Karen Novak benefit)

A note on sources:

The oral history was compiled mainly from interviews with the members of craw—as well as Darin Gray, Derek Hess and Aaron Turner—conducted by Hank Shteamer either in person, over the phone or via e-mail from 2010 through 2015. I would like to thank Adam Galblum for unknowingly kicking off the craw oral-history initiative by conducting the 1997 interview with David McClelland, which was originally slated for publication in Jim Ellis's *CLE Magazine* and is quoted in the *Map, Monitor, Surge* section above. Thanks as well to Mike Hill, whose 2014 interview with McClelland on his *Everything Went Black* podcast is also quoted.

The following articles were also consulted or quoted directly. When quoting, I've included the year of publication in order to distinguish these passages from the more recent material in the oral history

-HS, 2015

Bracelin, Jason. "Sonic Boon." Cleveland Scene. March 7, 2002.

Christe, Ian. "Craw: Rust-Colored Glasses." Alternative Press. March, 1994.

Heaton, Michael. "The Craw of the Wild." The Plain Dealer Sunday. July 20, 1997.

McLeod, Jeff. Interview with Rockie Brockway. The Subversive Workshop. Summer/fall, 1994.

West, Patrick. Interview with Neil Chastain and David McClelland. Change Zine. Spring, 1995.

Bibliography

Bataille, Georges. Guilty. Paris: Gallimard, 1961

Blakeslee, Sandra. "Complex and Hidden Brain in Gut produces Butterflies and Valium." The New York Times, (New York) January 23, 1996. B10

Bradbury, Ray. R is for Rocket. New York: Doubleday and Company, 1962.

Bradbury, Ray. S is for Space. New York: Doubleday and Company, 1966.

Capra, Fritjof. The Tao of Physics. New York: Shambhala Publications, 1975.

Frost, A. B. Stuff and Nonsense. New York: Charles Scribners and Sons, 1884.

Haykin, Simon. Communication Systems (2nd ed.). New York: John Wiley & Sons, 1983.

Joyce, James. Ulysses. New York City: Random House, 1946.

Larson, Erik. "The Story of a Gun." The Atlantic. January, 1993. pp. 48-78.

Lotringer, Sylvère; Virilio, Paul. Pure War. Los Angeles: Semiotext(e), 1983.

Marshall, Jonathan; Scott, Peter Dale; Hunter, Jane. The Iran-Contra Connection. Boston: South End Press, 1987.

May, John. The Greenpeace Book of the Nuclear Age. New York: Pantheon Books, 1989.

Perry, Tim; Glinert, Ed. Fodor's Rock & Roll Traveler USA. 1st Edition. New York: Random House, 1996.

Richards, Laura Elizabeth (Ed.) Four Feet, Two Feet, and No Feet; or, Furry and Feathery Pets, and How They Live. Boston: Estes and Lauriat. 1886.

Shulman, Seth. "Code Name: Corona." Technology Review. October, 1996. pp 22-32.

Virilio, Paul. Speed and Politics: an Essay on Dromology. Paris, France: Éditions Galileé, 1977.

Wertheim, Margaret. "Unnatural Appetites." The Sciences. May-June 1996. pp 15-17.

Wire Reports. "John Salvi Convicted in Clinic Murders: Receptionists Slain at Abortion Centers." The Plain Dealer (Cleveland) March 19, 1996. pg. 1.

Acknowledgments

Special thanks to Tom Abbs, Adam Downey and Chris Weiss at Northern Spy Records; to Eric Palmerlee and Johnathan Swafford at Aqualamb; and to David McClelland of craw. This release would not have been possible without their efforts.

Another special note of thanks goes to everyone who backed the craw reissue project on Kickstarter or helped spread the word about our fund-raising efforts. You are the real reason that this box set exists.

Thanks as well to Steve Albini, for engineering all three albums contained in this reissue; to Bill Korecky, for his work on *Map, Monitor, Surge* and many other craw recordings; and to the artists who contributed to the original packaging.

And thanks to Brendan Coyne and Phil Tory of Choke, Inc., for believing in craw, and for releasing *craw* and *Lost Nation Road* the first time around.

The following individuals were also invaluable to the craw reissue effort:

AIDA AMER
ROBERT BANKS
MILLIE BENSON
JOE BURNS
FRANK CASSIDY
ANDREW CRAWSHAW
JEREMIAH CYMERMAN
JOHN DELZOPPO
MARTIN GERAMITA
DARIN GRAY
BENJAMIN HAAS
DEREK HESS
MIKE HILL
DREW KATZ
KEITH MARLOWE
FRANKLIN MCCLELLAND
JEFF MCLEOD
KAREN NOVAK
KAREN OLLIS
ANASTASIA PANTSIOS
FRED PESSARO
HARRIET ROBERTS
NICK SAKES
DAN SCOFIELD
CHRIS SMITH
ETHAN SWAN
STEVE TULIPANA
AARON TURNER & HYDRA HEAD RECORDS
PATRICK WEST

Lastly thank you to all the members of craw for their participation and support:

CHRIS APANIUS
ROCKIE BROCKWAY
NEIL CHASTAIN
ZAK DIERINGER
DAVID MCCLELLAND
JOE MCTIGHE
WILL SCHARF

I would like to dedicate this release to these musicians, in the hopes that they realize their work made a difference. The sounds contained herein—and the individual and collective drive, passion and creativity that birthed them—have altered the life of this listener for the better. Thank you.

-H.S.
August, 2015

craw

choke inc.

www.ingramcontent.com/pod-product-compliance
Lightning Source LLC
Chambersburg PA
CBHW022105090426
42743CB00008B/721
* 9 7 8 0 6 9 2 5 6 5 7 3 5 *